Crystal
for health a

Crystal Massage
for health and healing

Michael Gienger

With contributions by

Hildegard Weiss
and
Ursula Dombrowsky

Translated from the German by
Tom Blair

Photography by
Ines Blersch

EARTHDANCER

A FINDHORN PRESS IMPRINT

Contents

To touch and be touched

To massage and to be massaged is one of the most special things in our lives. Who doesn't enjoy having nothing to do but put oneself in the hands of a trusted masseur or masseuse and simply let nice things happen? But giving the massage is equally pleasant. To give your best to a person who has put his or her trust in you, and to see how good it makes that person feel – what more could you want?

To massage means to touch (Arabic 'massa' = 'to touch'). And deep down we all long for someone to touch us. It is the foundation of every culture, every contact and every interaction. Just a glance, a word or a gesture can touch us. But direct skin contact is something very special. It is too bad that this direct skin contact is becoming rarer; in part this may be because we have less time; because we don't know how, or because we don't think of touching people other than those who are closest to us.

But a world without physical contact would be a much poorer world. By contrast, a world in which many people touch each other would be a world rich in contact, sympathy and understanding. I noticed how much I began to like the people I massaged during my time as a shiatsu practitioner. And frequent massages always allow our understanding for each other to grow, regardless of differences in our thinking, our behaviour or our lives.

In the Icelandic Edda we find this: 'A gift, and a gift in return, founds friendship, if nothing else opposes it'. Could there be a better gift, and gift in return, than touching each other?

It's no wonder, then, that massages are so beneficial; and not just for the body, but for the soul, mind and spirit too. To touch and be touched always has to do with the whole being – therefore every massage is holistic healing; and a healing form, by the way, that anyone can apply! For the essence of the massage is not the technique, but the turning to someone else, to a partner, with the intention of doing good, of providing a sense of wellbeing, and of healing. Our hands usually know by themselves what feels good and what has to be done, if we open ourselves to this kind of turning to someone. Following the instructions in a textbook accurately is much less important than *how* we do it, the spirit in which we offer a massage.

We would like to take you to a special world of massage with this book – massaging with crystals. Crystals and massage? This might seem a strange, even unpleasant, idea at first, because we always think of crystals as being hard, heavy, with rough edges – but you might be surprised at how 'soft' crystals can be, how delicate they are on our skin and body, and how much lightness they can provide us with. Crystal massage combines the advantages of massaging – the intensive tactile contact, and of crystal healing – the harmonious healing properties of crystals. The results are very subtle, and yet convey effective healing properties in various ways.

We can work on various levels – physical, ethereal, mental, spiritual; depending upon how we apply the crystals. The result, in the end, is always holistic, and yet every massage has a different point of access. Each one opens a different door to us, and to our inner world, metaphorically speaking. So I am particularly pleased to include the various contributions to this book; I am delighted that Ursula Dombrowsky and Hildegard Weiss were willing to introduce massage forms they have developed or enhanced themselves within its pages. Very interesting and versatile techniques have been developed in the young history of crystal healing.

I would also like to thank Marco Schreier, who was the initial inspiration for this book, and who let us dig deeply into his stock of crystals. I also owe thanks to Sabine Schneider-Kühnle for accompanying the project; to my publisher Andreas

performing massage in front of the camera. I would like to thank Eva-Lena Kurtz for assistance in the studio, as well as Steven Kielzsch and Michaela Wersebe for their contribution as models – especially Michaela for all of her patience, endurance and her excellent talent. This book would not be what it is without Ines Blersch's professional eye: she has succeeded in taking really enchanting photos. A sincere thank you for all the years of such good co-operation.

We would now like to invite you, the reader, to just try out the crystal massages that appeal to you. Whether professionally or for private use, make the most of the opportunity for a lovely exchange with your partner, friends and acquaintances – or apply crystal massages in your massage or naturopathy practice, if you work in a healing profession. Our experiences have been consistently positive: crystals give the massages additional healing effects, and massages provide us with a more intensive experience of the effects of healing crystals. And there is hardly anything more enjoyable than touching or being touched – in this case by both human hands *and* stones!

Michael Gienger

Lentz for his willingness to publish this book at a tangent to all of his schedules; Fred Hageneder for his sure instinct in design; Arwen Lentz for publishing this English edition; Tom Blair and Roselle Angwin for their work on this wonderful translation; Stefan Fischer for arranging for me to meet Michaela and Steven; Franca Bauer, Gabriele Simon, Dagmar Beck and Erik Frey for their best massage crystals, as well as Ewald Kliegel and my wife Anja Gienger for their dedication in

The basics of crystal massage for health and healing

Michael Gienger

*Crystal massages are the most enjoyable way
of experiencing the effects of healing crystals.
Such an experience broadens one's whole
pleasure in the gifts of the earth offered to us
in crystals, stones and gemstones.*

A moment of meeting

A massage is a special moment of meeting. It is therefore very important to devote proper time, space and attention to this moment: enough time to be able to enjoy the massage, and enough time for the massage to continue to have an effect. This means both the amount of time which we are whole-heartedly willing to give, and also the amount that our partner is willing to accept. Another important criterion is a pleasant and safe environment where both parties feel comfortable and undisturbed. We also have to be willing to be completely 'present', and to direct our undivided attention to the massage and to the person being massaged. This last is important because it is this 'being here' that creates the atmosphere of the massage, the 'inner room'– this can compensate for a lot if the outer conditions or situation are not ideal. It is still worth creating a pleasant 'outer room', though, because the massage and its effects will be longer lasting and more satisfying.

The 'outer room'

A warm, quiet place where you can give a massage undisturbed is the ideal place for a crystal massage. Warmth is very important, as the person who receives the massage will usually be unclothed (some areas of the body may be covered with a woollen blanket at the beginning but this is not always desirable). As the person being massaged is likely to be totally immersed in the experience, and sensitivity is heightened, any cover can be disturbing – one would like to enjoy the freedom! It is a good idea, therefore, to have a heater of some kind close by in case it is needed.

A well-designed room with a relaxing atmosphere also helps the person receiving the massage to let him- or herself go and to receive the massage better. A positive response to the ambience is half the massage.

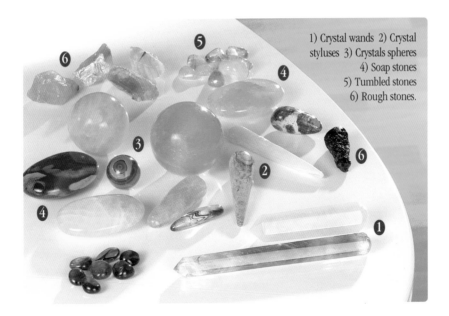

1) Crystal wands 2) Crystal styluses 3) Crystals spheres 4) Soap stones 5) Tumbled stones 6) Rough stones.

The treatment surface

A massage is administered on the floor on a firm mattress or on two or three woollen blankets covered with a sheet, forming a treatment surface. A massage couch is even better if available. The massage surface can differ, depending on the type of massage and the situation. Some people can relax better on the floor as they are not so 'close to the abyss'... For home massage, a bed can be used in principle, but mattresses that are too soft affect many massages because they make direct pressure difficult (the body gives way) or they make the changing of positions difficult because of the lack of resistance. Pillows, knee-rolls, woollen blankets and additional cushions should always be within reach during the massage.

Clothing

I recommend that the masseur or masseuse wear loose fitting, lightweight clothing because it does get pretty warm while treating, even though we hardly exert ourselves physically. The reason for this is that our energy also starts flowing strongly. (One of the advantages of massaging is that it is always good for both parties!) It is also helpful for both parties to drink a lot of pure water on the day of the massage (and, of course, to go to the bathroom shortly before the massage), so that the bodies' energy can flow well.

Crystals

We can use round tumbled stones ('worry' stones), crystal massage-wands, rods, round crystals, soap stones, lens-formed stones and many other forms, and in certain massages even rough stones, crystals and crystal-essences, as crystal massage aids. Crystal massage wands are usually hexagonal with a round base and a tip. They should be approximately eight to ten centimetres long for best handling. Crystal massage styluses look like long drops and therefore have a wider base and a thinner more pointed, slightly rounded end, and are eight to twelve centimetres long. The wider end has a more relaxing and comforting effect in some techniques and the more pointed end, in contrast, a more activating and vitalising effect.

Massage oil

Massage oil is usually not needed for crystal massages because the stone's polished surface slides well on skin, and the effect of some massage techniques (for example vital body massages) can even be slowed by oil. If you do work with oils you should generally use high-quality, natural, organic vegetable body-oils. Good oil can enhance the success of many massages, but low-quality oils slow and block the success.

Things you need for crystal massage for healing

1. A pleasant, safe and quiet room, if possible with a good ambience
2. A comfortable treatment surface (a mattress, woollen blankets, sheets, if available a massage couch or bed)
3. Comfortable, lightweight clothing
4. Warmth (a heater if available)
5. Pillows, knee-rolls, other such things for comfort
6. Blankets to cover up with (optional)
7. Tumbled stones, round stones, crystal rods, crystal wands or other stones
8. Massage oil (not for all massages).

The 'inner room'

Before you start a massage you should allow yourself and the person whom you are going to massage a few minutes to 'arrive'. A short conversation while having a glass of water or a cup of tea, then a short stop in the bathroom — and you're 'here' in a totally different way than you are if you immediately stumble towards the massage couch (especially directly after a car journey). The person you are going to massage should find a comfortable position at the beginning of the massage. Rest the recipient of your massage on pillows, cushions et cetera until he or she is totally comfortable, then cover him or her with a woollen blanket, if necessary. Allow the person (and yourself) a moment of peace and contemplation before you begin.

It is helpful for you to visualise that you are totally here for your client/partner during this time. Everything else is secondary while you are massaging – your everyday life, your problems, your interests; yes, even your own wellbeing. Consciously put it all aside, and direct your attention totally to the massage.

It is not only your hands that function while giving a massage, but also your thoughts, feelings and perceptions. Therefore they need to be collected, quiet, neutral and focused only on the wellbeing of your client or partner.

Protection

Before you begin, you should create a protective boundary, psychically, where everything that belongs to you stays within you, and everything that belongs to your partner or client stays within him- or herself, too. Energy should not be 'exchanged' during massages. 'Foreign' energy is always a weight. The goal of a massage is to dissolve tension and blocks and to let your own energy flow.

Flowing energy is available energy. Energy that does not flow is bound, blocked or is not free any more. If we have our own vital energy, we have such an amount of potential available that we don't need foreign energy. We all live by our own efforts.

You can create such a safe environment by determining that everything stays where it should, or returns to where it comes from.

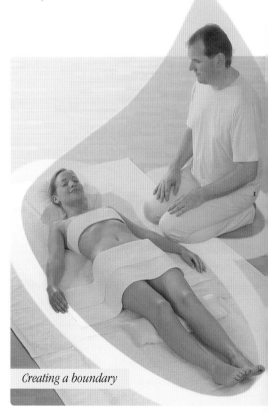

Creating a boundary

You can also imagine a violet flame around your client/partner and yourself this will have the same function. Visualising the symbol of a horizontal figure-of-eight (two circles that touch but are still separate) around your client/partner and yourself can also be helpful. Whatever you use to visualise a boundary, the most important thing is that the person you massage and yourself are always safe.

Sensing

Protected as you now are, you can consciously empathise with the person you are massaging at the beginning of the treatment. Our empathy is a sense as much as sight, hearing, smell, touch and taste. While massaging, we are especially dependent upon this sense, and a massage is especially good if you massage intuitively instead of simply 'technically'. It is not only about the sensitivity of our hands, either – both bodies can actually synchronise. One possible way of doing this is to breathe in the same rhythm as your client/partner. This way you are consciously 'in time' with them, which allows her or his body-feeling to be conveyed quickly. This may feel very unusual to you, but if you get into this feeling you will have a good sense of what is good for the person you are massaging, and what is not so satisfying. Don't worry

about returning to your normal breathing rhythm after one or two minutes (it might become strenuous otherwise); the empathy will remain if you want it to.

The beginning of a crystal massage for healing

You will need:

1. A comfortable position for the person being treated (pillows, cushions etc.)
2. Concentration and a clear direction of your consciousness only to the massage
3. To create a protective boundary (determine that everything stays where it should, or returns to where it comes from). If necessary visualise this (i.e. a mantle of light, a horizontal figure-of-eight)
4. To empathise with the person being massaged (by, for example, synchronising breathing).

Posture and position

We massage sitting or standing, depending on the position of the person to be treated – whether she or he is on the floor, or lying on a massage-couch. It is important in either case that we are in a comfortable position ourselves: a position in which we can both straighten up and lean forward to massage without effort. The right sitting position is important while working on the floor, and the correct height adjustment is important while massaging on the massage-couch (sturdy but adjustable beds are always preferable). Seating, posture and position will be discussed in the chapters pertaining to the various crystal massages. It is always advantageous if we begin in a centred position so that we can always return to our own centre.

> Always check at the beginning that you are in a position in which you can remain over a long period of time. Some massage positions are unusual, but many things can be rectified by a small correction of your posture or of your sitting position – this conserves a lot of strength.

Massage technique

The massage techniques – grips, movements and application of the crystals – differ widely in the various crystal massages introduced here, depending on which areas of the body are being massaged. We can generally say, though, that many applications are less strenuous and feel more pleasant if we let our whole body 'take part'.

We invite you here to try a little exercise. Sit in front of a table and push against the edge of the table with both thumbs. First do it with the strength of the muscles in your arms. The movement will be rela-

tively jerky and will continue through your whole body accordingly. No notable energy-flow develops and it soon starts to be strenuous.

Now push your thumbs against the edge of the table by shifting your body back and forth. Your arm-muscles only hold, but do not push, themselves. The movements are much more harmonious this way; pressure changes fluidly, a flow of energy develops in you, and it is hardly strenuous at all. Can you feel the difference?

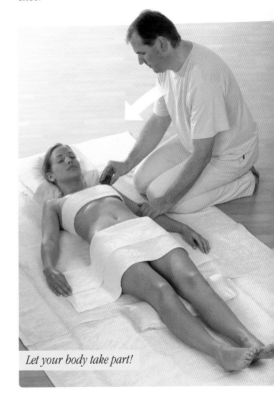

Let your body take part!

> Whether we do small fine movements as in vital body massage, or whether we use more pressure as in massages with round crystals, it is always helpful to let the movement be generated by the whole body, and to use gravity while leaning back and forth.

This does not only apply in massaging! Moving this way can save you from fatigue, tension, pain and many ailments. It is even easier and better if we co-ordinate movement and breathing: exhale while you perform the movement, especially while pushing, gripping or lifting. You can, for example, avoid backaches, or open tight screw tops, much more easily in everyday life in this manner. In massaging you can save energy and it will feel more pleasant. Inhale while you let go or if you pause in your movement. This might not be possible with all massage techniques, but where the rhythm of 'gripping' and 'letting go' exists (no matter how subtle) this breathing rhythm is very helpful. Once you are accustomed to this, you will automatically breathe like this (even in everyday life). I cured recurring backaches in my time as a paramedic using only this technique.

Attention

This 'technique' demands a lot of attention when we massage for the first time. This is perfectly normal. Simply keep remembering to direct your attention to the wellbeing of the person you are massaging. Facial expression, breathing, involuntary movements, bowel sounds (often a sign of relaxation) and voice sounds and utterances, of course, give you feedback on your massage. This feedback is very important to make sure we are on the 'right track'. The better your command of the massage technique, the more attention is freed for observation.

Presence

The danger of any routine, though, is that we don't actually stay present, but that we allow our minds to wander towards other things. We then just massage 'technically' and automatically, while we are absent spiritually. In this case the massage will not be deeply effective, even though we do everything correctly. It will be missing presence, atmosphere and *esprit*.

The solution to this is easy:

> Be aware of the need at all times to be totally 'here' spiritually, to devote yourself entirely to the massage and to keep your full attention on the person under your hands.

Reactions

Massages loosen things up – and everything that loosens initiates a reaction. It is reassuring, of course, if relaxation and wellbeing result from our crystal massage.

Sometimes, though, something that is in the way of lasting wellbeing has to be resolved. So don't be afraid of a client's moaning, sighing or even crying. Massages that produce these kind of reactions often bring the most relief. If you notice tense facial expressions or sounds of discomfort, don't hesitate to ask what is the matter. Some things just have to be expressed, and are then resolved. If tears begin to flow, ask if you should pause or if you should continue. You will usually be asked to continue; otherwise, just pause and continue once the crying is over.

> Crying is something positive, because it relieves. Please don't suffocate it by assuming the person needs consolation. Just remain 'present' and allow the tears to flow. It can be so good just to be allowed to cry...

Just wait until the tears have stopped flowing (and offer tissues if needed) and then go on with your crystal massage. Please do not stop at this point, if it is at all possible! You can be sure that 'sunshine always follows rain'! It's important always to

Notice the effect of the massage.

conclude massages at a 'good point'. This point will definitely arrive if you massage thoroughly, gently and sensitively, and are always 'totally there' for your client.

The good point

The so-called 'good point' is an important rule! This moment can, to all intents and purposes, occur before the planned conclusion of a crystal massage. Suddenly the person beneath your hands begins to breathe a sigh of relief, to smile joyfully, maybe even starts to laugh and finally to indulge in bliss. Can you do anything 'better'? Hardly! So the best thing to do is to stop at this point. Finish the area you are massaging at that moment (for example the second leg if you have only massaged one) but then conclude the crystal massage. As the recipient will go home in the state in which you finish the massage, clearly it needs to be the best possible state!

If you pass the high point, if the glow disappears again and the emotions of your partner seem to sink, you can ask them: 'Where was it best?' after you have completed an area. The recollection alone is sometimes enough to let the feeling return again immediately. If not, just ask: 'Should I massage that place once more?' If the answer is 'Oh yes', a short treatment of the area is usually sufficient to restore the 'good point'. If the answer is rather: 'No, please continue', then simply go on with the crystal massage. You will always find a way to the 'good point' as long as you are empathic and stay with the person you are massaging spiritually, and if you are not too shy to ask questions, if in doubt.

Finish at the 'good point'!

> The 'good point' can be defined as an 'improvement in comparison to the original state'. This is not necessarily an immediate state of the above-mentioned bliss, in most cases. Sometimes we can only accomplish small steps with a massage. Every improvement, whether small or large, is, nevertheless, a success. A 'good point' will have been achieved, in any case, even if the crystal massage were to continue indefinitely...

The carrying out of a crystal massage for healing

1. Find a comfortable position for yourself from which you can massage 'from your centre'
2. Let your whole body and gravity work for you and synchronise your breathing with your movements
3. Keep your attention solely on the massage and the person you are massaging
4. Allow reactions to arise. Give your client the necessary space and then continue with the massage. Do not suffocate tears with over-hasty consolation, they herald relief.
5. Finish the massage at a 'good point'.

The conclusion

It is best to stay in the room (physically and spiritually), just to be quiet and to observe how the person you have treated feels, at the conclusion of a crystal massage. Just stay seated close by and maybe ask how he or she is feeling. Be responsive to whatever is asked for, silence or to talk about the massage, to be left alone or to stay in contact. Give the person the space he or she needs, stay there or withdraw as is appropriate. You can say: 'Take the time you need and call me when you're ready', if you leave the room. You have then clearly agreed that there is enough room and time to let effects and feelings settle, as much as is desired.

Trading back of taken-over energy

You might remind yourself once more of the resolution that everything that belongs to you stays within you, and that everything that belongs to the person you have treated stays within him or her. You might envisage a short-term connection during which the exchange of energy can flow. Interestingly enough, you may often notice relief in yourself as well as in your counterpart. Cut the connection as soon as everything has been separated.

Trading back of taken-over energy

Spiritual release and clarification

There is a cleansing formula to clear the room if you still have the feeling that 'something' is still present, in you, in your partner or in the space around you. This indefinable 'something' you might sense could be energy that belongs to you or to the person you have massaged: alien ideas, views, emotions et cetera that would just otherwise just 'be stuck' in the room. Picture this 'something' as many small energy particles, and direct the following idea purposefully towards these particles: 'Return to the moment of your creation – or be free!' You might have to send this thought out a few times, but you will soon realise that what was left in the room has dissolved and disappeared.

> This final separation, clearing and dissolving of traded or absorbed energy is a great help in treatments and massages, so that you are not weighed down with someone else's energetic 'ballast'.

The observation that nothing is per se 'bad' or 'good', but that it is best for all things to be in the right place, or free, is helpful in this case. If you like, you can also cleanse your room with resonance spheres or bowls and tuning forks, or by using sage, incense or other means to smoke out the room; this all works in the same way. This 'mental cleansing', while the person you have treated is still here, can make sure that there is a good conclusion energetically.

Feedback

The feedback about the crystal massage is, naturally, very exciting and very interesting for both parties. Check to see if what the person you have treated reports corresponds with your observations. This is a good opportunity to learn and to sharpen your senses. But only speak about it directly after the massage if the treated person so desires. A forced conversation can undermine the success of the treatment. Otherwise just finish the present treatment and speak about the massage at a later time. Often perceptions of a crystal massage only come into consciousness some time afterwards, as the crystal massage gently continues to have an effect…

The end

You may slip out of your role as therapist once the massage and the succeeding conversation have been concluded completely. What you 'set aside' before may now be 'taken back' if you (still) want to. It is also good to leave the treatment room (at least for a short break) or to tidy it, to return it to its actual function (if you massaged at home, for example).

Effects of crystal massages are lasting

Cleansing

You should also cleanse the crystals you have used of the absorbed energy and information after the massage. Hold them under running water for a minute or longer, and rub them vigorously with your fingers. You will notice that the surface of the stones feel somewhat 'soapy' in the beginning, and then starts to build up resistance; after a while the rubbing finger

Cleansing the crystal

The conclusion of a crystal massage for healing

1. Be present, observe and ask about about the wellbeing of your client. Leave time and room for any needs
2. Trading back of taken-over energy (with the help of imagination if need be)
3. Dissolving of energy still stuck in the room: 'Return to the moment of your creation – or be free!'
4. Feedback and conversation about the massage (only if desired)
5. Deliberate letting go of your therapist role and return to 'everyday life'. If necessary, leave the room or clean up
6. Cleansing of the crystals under flowing water and with an amethyst (see below).

does not slide as well any more. That shows you that absorbed energy has been washed away. Take the crystals out of the water and lay them on an amethyst geode or a piece of an amethyst geode. The amethyst will free the stones of the last 'foreign' information. After a few hours your crystal will be cleansed, ready for your next treatment.

Possibilities and limits

Please do not give a crystal massage if you are unfit or unwell, or are not in a good mood!

As we mentioned before, it is not only your hands which effect the massage, but also your moods and thoughts. Choose therapies in which the influence is not so strong, like the 'laying on' of crystals, in such situations. You should always be able to remain neutral for crystal massages; just observing and doing what is best for your client. Do not let yourself be persuaded into giving a massage if you are not willing to, or if the basic conditions are not right. Otherwise you risk the results for both parties turning out to be unsatisfying. Please also note the possible restrictions and limits of the different types of crystal massage mentioned in the respective chapters.

The crystal massages mentioned in this book serve primarily as ways to achieve wellbeing and to mobilise self-healing forces. They have been proven and tested in practice, but are naturally not a substitute for diagnoses or treatments from doctors or alternative practitioners. You should always ask for competent advice if confronted with a serious condition, and only administer a crystal massage after consulting the treating specialists.

If you feel fit and wide awake, if there are no basic concerns and you enjoy and feel like massaging, you will be able to achieve wonderful results. The range of possibilities is massive – not only tired muscles, but also bones and joints can be made fit again with crystal massages. A multitude of other ailments as well as moods and mental problems can be influenced positively, too. You will find out more in the individual chapters.

Let's go...

The basic steps described in this introduction are performed similarly in all crystal massages. Some massage techniques restrict certain aspects or make them redundant, whereas others emphasise them. This is the nature of the work. It is very helpful to memorise these fundamentals – or to write them down as 'crib notes'. But don't simply copy the summaries noted above out of the book. That wouldn't help much, yet. Once you've noted down the respective keywords yourself, you'll remember them more easily when needed.

In the end, you learn to massage by massaging! Everything else develops by itself. It is an art that has to be practised and experienced. But the nice thing about massaging is that practising is fun for both parties, bringing happiness and wellbeing. Erich Kästner said 'For there to be good, you need to do it', and this is especially the case in massaging. So let's go…

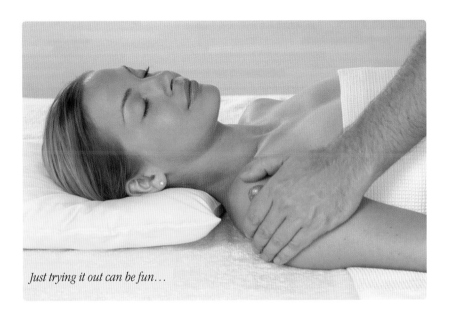

Just trying it out can be fun…

Intuitive massages with healing crystals

Michael Gienger

Intuitive crystal massages are more than 'simply' relaxing massages. Bringing massage and healing crystals together allows a deep effect to develop that influences body, soul, mind and spirit.

Intuitive healing crystal massage

Massaging feels good! The good thing about massaging is that success is almost certain if we proceed carefully and sensitively, and if we observe the results of what we are doing closely. You only need a few round polished crystals and some experience in the various massage techniques, apart from the basics we have already mentioned – so now we can start...

It is helpful to try out the different massage techniques with little massages on yourself first to experience this, so that you know the possibilities and limitations of different applications so that you can apply these correctly. Once you have experienced how various massage techniques feel on yourself at least once, the appropriate movements will come unerringly naturally in later massages.

A small preparatory exercise

So try the following massage: make movements with the crystals on the inner skin of your forearm, your chest and abdomen or on your thigh – somewhere that you can massage yourself effectively and comfortably.

Circling: Move the crystal across the skin in circular motions applying more and less pressure alternately. Try out the differences between small and large circles and differing speeds as well as the difference between the flat surfaces and (rounded) edges of the crystal.

Circling

Rubbing: Guide the stone over the skin in long straight movements, putting pressure on the surface evenly. Differences result from the variation of pressure, speed and the area being massaged.

Rubbing

Pulling: Pulling is similar to rubbing, except that it is applied to smaller areas and more pressure is put onto the 'back end' of the stone (in relation to the direction of movement). Vary pressure and speed with the area being massaged.

Pulling

Joggle: Moving the crystal back and forth dynamically, while rubbing or pulling, firmly joggles body parts and muscles. A strong loosening movement that needs a certain pressure and speed but must not be too firm. Try it out!

Joggling

Vibrating: The stone is moved up and down dynamically while rubbing or pulling, so that the muscles and body parts vibrate over a large area. You may also vibrate in just one spot for a short time. Experiment to find out what amount of pressure and speed is the most agreeable.

Vibrating

Kneading: Muscles and tissue are worked over with firm pressure and with turning movements here. Try out the minimum pressure and the 'comfortable maximum limit'.

Kneading

Pressing: The crystal is pressed into the muscles briefly and firmly, then moved on without pressure, and pressed again. A line of several pressure points is formed this way. Pressing is an enjoyable and simultaneously deeply loosening technique. It is very important here not to apply pressure using muscle power whilst massaging someone, but only by shifting your weight (see chapter 'The basics'). ⇒

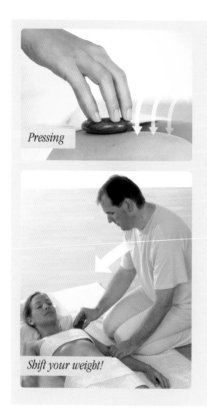

Pressing

Shift your weight!

Drumming: Rhythmic, soft drumming of the body surface with the stone results in a vitalising effect. Try to vary the speed, strength and area massaged.

Drumming

There are a number of very different possibilities and variations on massaging with a healing crystal. The techniques described aren't all of them by any means – you can develop additional ideas yourself with a little imagination and creativity. Try various techniques out with a partner, taking turns at massaging, and familiarise yourself with them. Once you have developed a feeling for the basic techniques, the right one will occur to you at the right point, during an intuitive massage.

The sequence of an intuitive healing crystal massage

First of all lay out the stones you feel will be suitable for carrying out a crystal massage (more in the following chapters). Then let your massage partner find a comfortable position (it is sometimes best to massage back and limbs first to practise) then ready yourself by, for example, breathing in the same rhythm as your partner.

Then just let the massage happen. See where your impulse leads you: are the shoulders crying out for relaxation? Is it the abdomen that hurts? Are the legs or feet tired? Sometimes you have the sense that you know exactly where to start. Follow this feeling; or else just begin with the back – this almost always feels good.

Now take the stone that 'jumps to your attention', the stone which your eyes fix on, the stone you just 'see/know/feel' will be right. Make contact with the area, let your hand rest there with the crystal and follow the motion that seems to happen by itself, or that is the easiest to carry out. This can be gentle circling, rubbing, pulling, joggling, vibrating, kneading, or drumming, whatever (see above)...

> Basically, any movement is all right in intuitive healing crystal massage if you

> feel that it fits, and it makes your counterpart feel good! (In my experience, though, pulling motions are usually more pleasant than pushing ones.)

Now massage the entire area using alternating techniques, in any way that comes to mind. Always observe the reactions of your partner at the same time. Tense muscles may hurt and need a certain amount of pressure to be loosened, so always make sure to provide relaxation and wellbeing in between the firmer massaging.

> Alternating between firm and gentle massage techniques makes a crystal massage dynamic and vivid. The aim is to create a pleasant and harmonious body tension that causes neither limp nor tense results from the variation between tension and relaxation. This basic body tension is the foundation of a healthy, vital body feeling.

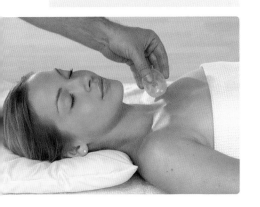

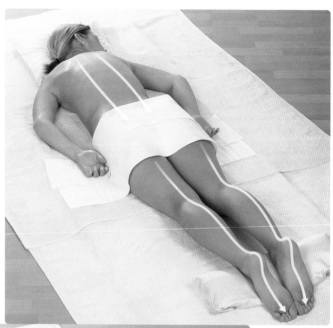

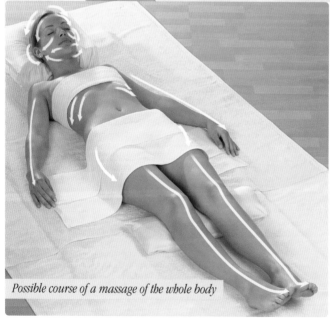

Possible course of a massage of the whole body

Bring some variety into the massage. The state we are hoping to achieve with the massage is similar to that of a cat crouching: the state of tension in every muscle is related to a deep peace that can last for hours – but is still capable of a reaction as fast as lightning. Cats are teachers of litheness!

It is usually best for the back, legs and feet if you massage them from top to bottom. This relaxes and dissolves pain. If someone's body is very un-toned, though, exactly the opposite direction might be helpful so, follow your intuition. Massaging the arms is similar to massaging the back and legs: it is usually more enjoyable if you work from the shoulders to the hands – but this rule is not without its exceptions, either.

'Downward and outwards' motions that follow the course of the ribs are recommended for the chest. Gentle techniques applied clockwise are used for the abdomen; this motion follows the course of the intestines. Rubbing motions are usually very pleasant for the skull and the nape of the neck. Gentle circling, kneading or pushing motions alternating with outward rubbing movements are good for the face.

It is not necessary, of course, always to do a massage of the whole body. Less is often more, especially when you are still practising. Do not overstrain yourself and only massage for as long as you have enough power, stamina and attention. If you notice that you are losing concentration or are getting tense, then finish massaging the respective area and close the session.

It is important, though, that you always complete the area you have begun. If you have massaged one side of the body massage the other side too. Also, always complete both legs, or both arms, otherwise a disturbing or unpleasant feeling of imbalance often remains.

could have happened, quietly and privately. If you notice that your massage client is feeling well, then you have done a good job of giving your massage!

It is also important in intuitive healing crystal massage that you leave time for your client to rest and enjoy the after-effects (if desired), and to ask how he or she feels after the massage, as described in the previous chapters. And please think about the trading back of taken-over energy, purifying of the room and the cleansing of the massage crystals that were used.

Holding the crystals

In principle, you should hold the stones in your hand firmly but not in such a way as to feel cramped while massaging. You should have the feeling that you have the stone 'safely under control'. Security or insecurity in holding the stones is transmitted to the person being massaged! Don't handle the crystals too casually either; 'casualness' can be misinterpreted as being neglectful. It is worth trying all this out with a client.

I would like to dwell on massaging with lens- and soap-formed crystals, which are often used in intuitive massages, here, to exemplify the holding and applying of

stones using different techniques. In principle, basically any stone with polished surfaces that doesn't have sharp edges can be used for crystal massages. However, lens- and soap-formed stones have a multitude of different application possibilities, unlike tumbled stones (unevenly polished pocket stones).

Lens-formed stone (c. 45 by 35 mm)

Soap-formed stone (c. 70 by 50 mm)

Lens- and soap-formed stones are flat, oval, polished massage crystals. Soap-formed stones are somewhat larger (approx. 50x75 mm), lens-formed stones are somewhat smaller (approx. 30x45mm). Both variations are slightly curved and pleasantly rounded on the edges. Soap-formed as well as lens-formed stones are available in many stone types today (see the following); the choice is somewhat more limited in soap-formed stones, though, because the mineral sometimes does not deliver raw stones that are large enough.

Massage techniques using lens- and soap-formed crystals

Harmonising: Firm motions with the flat side of a soap-formed stone (circling, pulling, kneading or pressing) on the skin have a harmonising effect. Hold the stone on its edge or by placing your entire hand on its surface so you can guide it and vary the pressure.

Harmonising

Stimulating: Motions on the skin with the 'narrow' (more rounded) edge are stimulating. This application is very invigorating even if you rub, circle or pull with little pressure. Hold the stone in your hand tightly and securely.

Stimulating

Energising: Joggling and vibrating with soap-formed crystals has an energising effect, and an even more stimulating effect. It is advisable to use the flat side of the stone because the edges might feel too intense, though this is not always the case.

Energising

Soothing rubbing: Rubbing with the flat side of the soap-formed stone always offers a relaxing and soothing element during the massage, and especially at the conclusion. The crystal is held more loosely and placed on the body more gently.

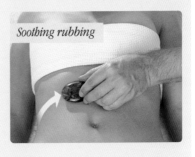
Soothing rubbing

Vitalising rubbing: Rubbing with the wide side of the crystal also has a relaxing effect, but is simultaneously vitalising. It awakens, stimulates the feelings and is good for the conclusion of the massage, if you want your client to go back into everyday life on an animated note.

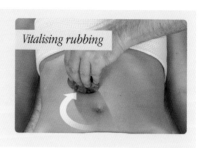

Vitalising rubbing

Selection of various massage stones:
(1) Crystal (2) Lens-formed stone
(3) Soap-formed stone (4) Crystal sphere
(5) Egg-formed stone (6) Disc-formed stone
(7) Thumb-formed stone (8) Tumbled stone

Playing with crystals and forms

Play with the forms – if you massage with lens- or soap-formed stones, round-polished tumbled stones, smooth raw stones or other forms! Irregularly-formed stones in particular have their peculiarities that are worth exploring. As time goes by, you will be able to assemble your special personal massage set out of various healing crystals.

The effect of the forms is complemented by the effect of the mineral content of the various healing crystals. It is sometimes amazing how different one and the same massage technique feels if we use orange calcite during one massage, then rose quartz, rock crystal or sodalite during following massages. The differences are enormous even if the stones are all exactly the same form. One stone, for instance, might tickle, whilst another cools, the third warms, the fourth vitalises, the fifth relaxes, the sixth upsets, and you might not be able to stand the seventh! These reactions are very individual, which means that they can differ from person to person, but this does show clearly that the healing properties of crystals can be felt directly!

The following description of the effects of the individual stones can only offers clues to the reactions often observed. This is not a guide to everything that is possible in individual cases. Try different crystals out – we are talking about intuitive crystal massage here!

The effects of the various massage crystals

 Agate gives you a good bodily sensation, a gentle feeling of being enveloped and protected by your own skin. It helps the metabolism of the connective tissue, and is therefore good for the skin.

 Agate in its more filigree form **lace agate** is very good for the supply and waste disposal of the connective tissue, as well as for the arteries and intestines. It brings finesse, mobility and spiritual flexibility.

 Agatised Coral (Petoskey-Stone) as a massage stone helps to gently reduce deeply-rooted tension. Coral helps one cope with difficulties, and with integrating oneself into social groups.

 Alabaster (orange) strengthens tissues and loosens stiff muscles. It helps one to define oneself, and stabilises unstable psychological states. Orange-coloured stones also help to heal infections.

 Amazonite is a wonderful massage stone for joint problems with different causes (stress, rheumatism, infections, liver conditions etc.). Amazonite also balances moods.

 Amethyst eases tension and gives you inner peace. More intensive massages can churn up the emotions at first bringing out sadness and grief. Physically, amethyst is good for skin and nerves.

 Anthophyllite is very good for the kidneys and ears. Massages around the ears can help against tinnitus or other ailments. It also helps resolves stress and to protect nerves.

 Aquamarine is very good for tired or aching eyes if you massage the area around the eyes with it. Used regularly it also helps prevent cross-eyedness and regulates near- and far-sightedness.

Aventurine encourages relaxation and sleep and helps heart conditions, stress and nervousness. It is also effective for infections, sunburn, and sunstroke if you massage using gentle strokes.

 Banded Amethyst relieves tension and headaches, soothes itching and sunburn (rub and pull only lightly for sunburn) and is helpful for people suffering from chronic fatigue.

 Blue Quartz (Blue Aventurine) cools and calms, helps nervousness, lowers blood pressure and curbs high pulse rates. It helps chronic tension and soothes pain.

 Calcite (blue) calms and encourages inner stability and security at the same time. It is very good for the lymph, skin, colon, connective tissue, bones and teeth (massage the jaw!).

 Calcite (orange) warms, vitalises and brings excellent bodily feelings (coenesthesia). It is very effective for the entire abdomen as well as for connective tissue, skin, joints and bones.

 Chalcedony (as Blue-Banded Crystal) activates body fluids, especially the lymph glands, kidney and bladder activity. Lowers high blood pressure.

 Dalmatian Stone (Aplite) has a strengthening, constructive and emotionally balancing effect. A massage crystal for balanced firmness and flexibility, for stable nerves and good reaction capabilities.

 Dumortierite gives serenity and lightness (the 'take-it-easy' stone), and is helpful as a massage crystal for pain, cramps, headaches, nervousness, motion sickness, even for nausea and vomiting.

Falcon's Eye (Blue Tiger's Eye) brings you 'back to earth' in crisis situations, helps you to see things objectively and to attain the proper distance, it eases restlessness, nervousness, shivering, pain and regulates over active hormones.

Fluorite (as multicoloured 'Rainbow Fluorite') is good for skin, tissue, bones and joints. It eases chronic tension, enables physical mobility and helps posture problems. Fluorite activates the nerves.

Gagate (Jet) is very good for mouth, digestion, intestines, skin, joints and spine. Facial massages can ease bruxism (grinding or clenching of the teeth), abdominal massages, and have a regulating effect on the intestines (also helpful for diarrhoea).

Girasol Quartz as a massage crystal makes you quiet, balanced, open and able to work under pressure. Massages around the eyes strengthen vision.

Heliotrope is the echinacea of crystals. It strengthens the body's defences, eases infections and helps early heart conditions. Heliotrope helps us to define and gather ourselves.

Hematite gives power and vitality. It vitalises, making the blood circulate and warms, makes the person active and burning for action. Physically it encourages haematopoiesis and oxygen transportation, and provides for vitality here too.

Jasper (Red Jasper or Brecciated Jasper) activates circulation and helps deal with weakness and exhaustion. It circulates blood, warms and gives energy. Red jasper especially boosts courage and the ability to assert oneself.

Kabamba Jasper is very good for the skin. It opens pores, encourages perspiration and the detoxification that comes with this. A very good massaging crystal to use in the sauna and before purification baths.

Labradorite is cooling on the one hand, but helps people who are shivering or who are sensitive to the cold. It reduces blood pressure and eases rheumatic conditions.

 Landscape Jasper assists digestion and excretion (stomach, pancreas and intestines), strengthens the spleen and the cleansing of connective tissue. Mentally, it gives constancy and endurance.

 Lapis Lazuli is very good for sore throats of any kind, calms nerves, and has a cooling and vitalising effect simultaneously. It helps us confide in others and to gain control over our lives.

 Larvikite (Syenite) helps heal heavy emotional disturbance, making you sober and neutral. It also calms the nerves, encourages purification of tissues, has a cooling effect and reduces blood pressure.

 Leopard Skin Jasper (Rhyolite) activates digestion and excretion and helps with skin problems and hardened tissue. It balances activity and rest and improves sleep.

 Magnesite has a deeply relaxing effect and helps with cramps and all kinds of pains. It eases headaches, migraines, sore muscles, stomach problems, nausea, back disorders and shooting pain.

 Mookaite gives a good body feeling (coenesthesia), because it has simultaneously a relaxing and vitalising effect. It makes you soft and strong at the same time, encourages blood purification and strengthens the spleen, liver and immune system.

 Moss Agate activates lymph flow and the cleansing of tissue, mucous membranes and the respiratory tract. It loosens inner tension, and is liberating if you feel heavy, depressed and constricted.

Obsidian (Snowflake Obsidian) helps pain, mental and physical blocks, dysfunctions of blood circulation or chronically cold hands and feet. It has a vitalising and spontaneously motivating effect, mentally.

 Ocean Agate (Ocean Jasper) tightens tissue, encourages lymph flow, detoxification and the immune system, eases infections and retards the growth of cysts and tumours. Gives courage to face life, and have hope.

 Onyx Marble is very good for the spine, the intervertebral discs, meniscus and joint disorders. It helps in cases of intense mental strain, and in situations that develop too quickly.

 Petrified Wood makes stable and helps us to be in our 'own centre'. It relaxes and fortifies, strengthens digestion, purifies and helps in cases of overweight due to a lack of 'grounding'.

 Prase helps with bladder ailments, eases pain, bruises and swelling, is cooling and reduces fever and helps for sunburn and sunstroke (stroke gently). Prase calms hot-tempered types.

 Rhodonite is very good for the muscles, connective tissue and circulation. It helps heart conditions and aids the healing of scars and old wounds. Rhodonite helps us to let go, to forgive and to start anew.

 Rhyolite (Rain Forest Jasper) is very good for the skin and subcutis, aids purification and therefore eases colds and infections. Mentally, rhyolite helps us to accept ourselves as we are.

 Rock Crystal cools and refreshes, has a liberating and loosening effect, but also revitalises. Rock crystal eases pain, opens up the senses, wakens and makes one clear, receptive and aware.

Rose Quartz improves sensibility and body feeling. It is good for the heart and aids blood circulation in the tissues. Rose quartz makes you aware of your needs, and therefore may be relaxing at one time and stimulating at another.

Ruby-Kyanite-Fuchsite is very rare but very valuable (in a crystal healing sense): this is a combination of three minerals that help paralysis, rheumatism, afflictions of the skin, heart and back ailments.

Schorl (Black Tourmaline) helps to reduce tension and enables the person to be composed and neutral. It alleviates pain and tension, in energetic terms Schorl unblocks scar tissue and helps kinetic disorders, paralysis and numbness.

Selenite (Fibre Gypsum) tightens tissue and eases pain, especially from overexertion. Mentally, it calms you when you are irritable and hyperactive, just when you think you are about to 'lose it'.

Septarian helps intestinal, skin ailments, and hyperacidity. Septarian loosens hardening and tumour-growths in tissue, and help you to open up.

Serpentine ('China Jade' or 'Silver Eye') is strongly relaxing and helps nervousness, unease and the feeling of being unprotected. It alleviates cardiac arrhythmias, kidney, stomach and menstrual disorders.

Smoky Quartz eases pain and helps to reduce tension caused by stress, especially headaches, neck and back problems and tense jaw muscles. Smoky quartz gives strength when someone is under constant pressure.

Sodalite cools, eases heat-sensitivity, reduces fever and blood pressure and helps sore throats and hoarseness. It liberates you when you have the feeling that you are being prevented from shaping your own life.

Stromatolite is very good for the intestines and helps the feeling of stomach pressure (also for worries). Stromatolite encourages metabolism and excretion and strengthens connective tissue and skin when used as a massage crystal.

Tiger's Eye gives calmness when everything 'goes haywire', helps one gather oneself, and attain perspective. It eases the consequences of stress and pain, and helps one be totally with oneself (rather than 'beside oneself').

Tiger Iron mobilises the 'tiger in your tank' and gives drive, dynamism and a lot of energy. Tiger iron encourages haematopoiesis and blood circulation and physically activates the circulation. Activates exhausted people.

All the healing crystals mentioned are available as special massage crystals, especially in the aforementioned forms: soap- and lens-formed crystals, but to some extent also as so-called life-stones (oloides), disc-formed crystals, thumb-formed crystals, pocket crystals and, naturally, as round-polished tumbled stones (worry stones). All of these forms can be used for intuitive healing crystal massage.

Vital body massage with healing crystals

Michael Gienger

Vital body massage is a gentle ethereal treatment, which works directly on the energetic level of the person being treated.

What is the vital body?

Vital body massage concentrates on treating the whole person at the energetic level, rather than treating the physical body alone. The massage consists of very gentle touching of the skin, with the intention of harmonising and vitalising the energy field that encircles and penetrates the body. This field is also called the etheric body, the vital aura, the morphic field, the subtle body or the vital body.

This energy field develops from the communication flow between our cells, tissue and organs, as well as between the organism and its soul, mind and spirit. Every cell – taken on its own – is an autonomous creature with its own consciousness. Each cell, after all, controls its own breathing, metabolism, regeneration and reproduction. Just imagine if you had to constantly give billions of cells orders. It is better that they take care of these affairs themselves, isn't it? So insofar as every cell has its own consciousness, it also has a desire to live; it has experiences, knows pain, knows activity and relaxation. When several cells join together to form tissue, the same consciousness, basically, pertains to this larger entity; the same thing applies when tissues join to form an organ and, of course, again in the fusion of organs to form an organism.

In vital body massage we assume that each aspect of our being – every cell, all tissue, every organ and our organism as a whole – has its own consciousness. Our body and every area in it knows exactly what it needs and what it does not need, what does it good and what harms it. The body has its own intelligence!

Why aren't we constantly healthy? Easy: because we listen to our body too rarely! Our body, for instance, signals satiation – and we keep on eating because it tastes so good (or because we were taught to leave our plate empty!). Our body signals fatigue – but we stay up and zap through the television programmes, hoping that we might find something interesting. Our body signals thirst but instead of serving it water, we serve it beverages that make it even thirstier (coffee, soft drinks et cetera).

This list could be extended indefinitely. So it isn't our body's fault when we become ill (it is doing its best), it's our fault! Our body compensates for many of our 'sins' every day; it can do so because it is extremely talented at self-organisation!

This organisation is only possible with communication. Needs have to be expressed, orders have to be transmitted, necessary things must be requested, finished goods must be managed, procedures have to be co-ordinated and plans have to be monitored. The logistics of these dimensions can only be accomplished with quick and goal-oriented communication; all the more so because the 'organisation' has trillions of 'employees'. The physical communication channels – nerves, blood and lymph channels – are not sufficient for this load. Our body also has energetic communication channels (meridians, biophotones) and even telepathic networks (thought connections).

The latter are not limited to our own body. On the contrary, we feel how someone else is doing without anything being said, with their help. Our telepathic impulses impart, for example, an uneasy feeling when something menacing comes our way, or a sense of joyful wellbeing when someone thinks about us in a loving way. A major part of the self-organisation of our body is taken care of on this level; that is why thoughts and emotions affect it so directly. And that is not all: the co-ordination of body, soul, mind and spirit also takes place this way.

The vital body is the sum of all energetic connections and communication processes in and around our body. The constant exchange via these connections and communications channels is simply vital. This is the reason that this communication and energetic field is called 'vital body' (Latin: 'vita' = 'life'). It is this field that keeps the body alive.

Can you perceive the vital body?

We can, if we look just beyond our skin (for example over our arm), perhaps sense a fine field around our body, similar to the

The vital body

47

Energy-rich and energy-poor areas
of the vital body

cold areas, that differ distinctly from the actual skin temperature!

The vital body can be seen as similar to a magnetic field. If we approach the skin carefully, a slight resistance that lets our hand spring back can be felt. Ticklish people sometimes react to this touching of the vital body with involuntary laughter, even without skin contact! You can even make the vital body 'audible', with a tuning fork or with resonance spheres (the sound of the resonating tuning fork or sphere changes as you enter and exit the vital body, or when you move it around in it).

Try to sense your own or someone else's vital body, preferably at twilight. Let your eyes blur just beyond your skin; it might help to half-close them. Then run your hands over the body at a distance of a few centimetres from the skin or test the sound changes with a tuning fork or resonance sphere. With a little practice you will be able to sense many nuances.

reflection of air over a hot road, during the day (it appears more like a fine white mantle during twilight). This is our vital body, our aura or morphic field, projecting above our physical body by a few centimetres. We can also feel it if we run our hand back and forth, gently and empathically, over someone else's skin, keeping a distance of a few centimetres. We can sense fine temperature differences, warm to hot, and cool to even

People who see auras often describe the vital body as a bright, white or sometimes light yellow field that envelops the body at a distance of two to ten centimetres. Lighter and darker areas can often be seen in this field (it also sometimes seems as if it disappears in the darker areas); the expansion

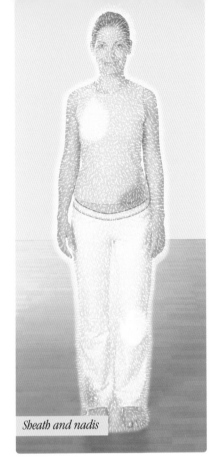

Sheath and nadis

Swirling energy in the vital body

over the borders of the body is not even, either. Light areas reflect energy-rich areas, whilst dark areas reflect energy-poor areas, which often correspond with the inner state of the respective body zones.

A well-developed ability to see auras lets you see even finer textures in the vital body. You may see countless very fine channels that run from within to without and open in the form of a funnel. These channels are also called 'nadis' (Sanskrit: 'nadi' = 'nerve, energy channel') in the tradition of ayurveda: they depict energetic exchange points with the environment. You may also see a gentle flow of inconspicuously flickering and slightly opalising energy in the whole vital body, comparable to a swirling water surface or the atmospheric swirl in the gas mantle of the planet Jupiter. Countless small swirls that rotate clockwise and counter-clockwise envelop our body. In doing so, however, they do not remain static. They become smaller and larger, and change their position and their direction of rotation, too. It is a flexible and lively field that envelops our bodies. The speed of the swirls varies, interestingly enough, and not always in connection with the lighter or darker areas.

Traditional Chinese medical science says: 'Life is change, standstill is death'. Accordingly, fast swirls in the vital body signify fast change, slow swirls slow change. Wellness does not depend on our energy levels alone, but rather on how we maintain our ability to change. This willingness to change is not synonymous with either a lot of energy (light areas), or little energy (dark areas).

By the way, nine larger swirls that are relatively 'true to their location', appear on the front and back of our body, from the tailbone/pubic bone to the parting in our hair, along our central body axis, amidst these many small swirls. These swirls are the expression of nine energy centres and are called chakras (in Sanskrit: 'Chakra' means 'turning wheel'). They can rotate in different directions like the other energy centres. Clockwise movements are, generally, compression and building-up

processes, counter-clockwise movements are dissolving and decomposition processes. Both processes are vital!

There is no good or bad associated with the direction of turn here, whether the rotation is to the right or to the left: 'good' is anything that supports or encourages the natural movement of the vertebrae, 'bad' in contrast is anything that retards and blocks – no matter in which direction!

This swirling and flowing can also be sensed. Touch the skin very carefully with your index and middle finger of one hand and start a gentle circling motion. Change direction after two to three circles. You will now notice that the motion is distinctly easier in one direction than the other. Follow this easier, more effortless direction of rotation. Keep your hand circling while you move it slowly over the skin. Suddenly the rotating direction of your fingers will reverse at some point. Now it is easier in the other direction. Soon you will experience another change of direction (and so on). Keep moving your fingers… You see how simple it is to sense the swirls and flow of the vital body – and if you continue, you will be carrying out a vital body massage already!

So we follow the natural stream and flow of the morphic field when applying a vital body massage. We do not deliberately initiate a change, but adjust to the already existing movements. We leave the direction to the body, trusting in its wisdom by supporting the existing energy flow. This improves the communication with and in the body, activates, vitalising, and strengthening the self-healing forces.

That is all we have to do. Basically, we just facilitate the function and communication of the body. But the effects are very good!

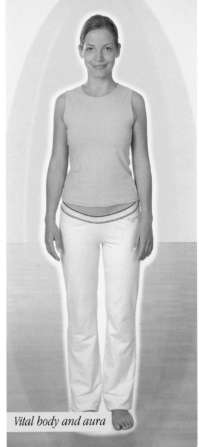

Vital body and aura

Vital body massage

The vital body is a part of what is often called the 'aura' ('vibrancy', from the Greek 'aura' meaning 'a breeze, haze'). It is the inner layer of the aura, which expresses the vitality of the body and affects it. Further layers of the aura are the gorgeous colourful emotional or astral body that can project a good arm's length or more beyond the body, and which reflects psychic impulses with its play of colours; and the mental body, which can be room-filling in its clear, clouded, foggy or free quality, and which reflects our thinking. Finally there is the invisible causal body, corresponding with our spiritual space.

Vital body massage does not actively treat these additional auric layers. But you

51

can observe that vital body massage influences them indirectly. The glow of the emotional body becomes lighter and more true-coloured, the mental body becomes clearer and freer and the person being treated almost always experiences that their spiritual space enlarges. Vital body massage reaches not only the body but also affects the soul (feeling), the mind (thinking) and the spirit (inner being).

Vital body massage can produce significant metamorphosis in all areas of our character, and, for this reason, is a holistic massage that simply supports the process of change. These metamorphoses might correspond with that which we really desire in our life. We can see that this is the case by looking at one factor: a dramatic improvement in the person's wellbeing!

What are the origins of vital body massage?

Massage has now been accompanying me for half of my life. I began a five-year shiatsu massage course when I was twenty years old, first with Martin Stotz and then with Andre Uebele. I then worked as a shiatsu masseur at the end of the 'eighties. I acquired knowledge of vital body massage and other etheric treatment forms

from Waltraud Ferrari, a student of the druid Raborne. The idea of performing this massage, that is actually carried out with the index and middle fingers, with crystals came spontaneously to me at the beginning of the 'nineties, at a time when I had already been using healing crystals for a while. The crystal wands available then in rock crystal, amethyst and rose quartz, which I knew of from acupressure massage, made me curious as to what might change in the area of vital body massage through using them here too. It was, initially, simply an experiment among friends – with exciting results.

The first vital body massages with crystals immediately showed that this is a wonderful way of experiencing the effect of crystals comprehensively and dramatically. In addition to the opening and liberating effect of the massage itself, a sensation as if one were 'filling oneself' with the information of this stone was felt when using a crystal wand or stylus. The physical, psychic, mental and spiritual qualities of the stone were sensed directly by both the people who were being treated and the people offering the treatment. Many symptoms disappeared almost magically – and in many cases permanently! We were astonished ourselves at the powerful effects of this seemingly-gentle treatment.

In the early nineties as vital body massage was developing you could really only find quartz crystals as crystal wands or styluses (rock crystal, amethyst, ametrine, smoky quartz and rose quartz). Ewald Kliegel is to be thanked for the fact that various additional crystal types were made into the practical stylus form that he uses for his reflex-zone massage with crystal styluses towards the end of the nineties. These 'new types' have also entered the domain of vital body crystal massage, but the emphasis is still on the use of quartz crystals, especially rock crystal.

Vital body massage with a crystal stylus

Experience from many different massage practices comes together in the form of vital body massage with crystals as it is practised today: its basis is still the druidic vital body massage, supplemented by experience from other ethereal treatment forms like reiki (building up of energetic protection), shiatsu (relieving posture through massage on the acupuncture points), reflex-zone massage (working with a stylus) and, of course, healing crystal treatment (effects of healing crystals).

Rock crystal is often used for non-specific treatments to relax, vitalise, clear and liberate without being targeted at a specific condition. It just gives energy (the correct amount), and clarity; things that one practically always needs.

Rock crystal massage stylus

After fifteen years of practice, vital body massage with healing crystals has developed into a holistic method that can be administered by anyone – if carried out accurately. It is, of course, better, as in any massage form, to learn this in its practical form, instructed by an experienced teacher (see addresses in the appendix). This chapter explains the basics, possibilities and limits of the massage sufficiently for you to be able to approach its application playfully (with partners, friends and relatives). It is certainly no problem for professional masseurs or masseuses to integrate vital body massage with healing crystals into their own repertoire.

How is vital body massage administered?

It is best to administer a vital body massage in a warm, quiet room, or outdoors. Warmth is very important, though, because vital body massage is a massage of the entire body; its effects develop directly on the skin, and sometimes it has a cooling effect because it has the tendency to enlarge the vital body as 'energetic space'. (However the ethereal activation of the vital body sometimes has the effect that blankets of any kind are unwanted – one wants to enjoy the freedom that develops!)

It is best to massage on the floor, where a mattress or two to three blankets, covered with a sheet, form a treatment surface on which the person being treated as well as the masseur or masseuse have enough room.

Crystals in the form of crystal wands, crystal stylus or longish tumbled crystals (round-polished 'worry' stones) are used for vital body massage. The broad rounded end as well as the pointed, slightly rounded end of the massage wands and styluses are used. The wide end has a more relaxing and calming effect, and the more pointed end, in contrast, has a more activating, vitalising effect. There is no qualitative difference between wand and stylus. Choose the form according to your personal preferences, or else by what is available in the respective crystal type.

Crystal wand, crystal stylus and longish tumbled crystal ('drop') of amethyst

We do not use massage oil for vital body massage. This would change the skin's surface and diminish the effects of the massage. Just let the person you are going to massage find a pleasant position – first in the face-down position and then in the dorsal position – and lay pillows, cushions et cetera under him or her until he or she is totally comfortable. It is best if he or she is unclad as much as possible because vital body massage only works on the skin. Allow the person a moment of peace and collection at the beginning.

> It is important during the vital body massage for you to protect yourself and the person being treated and to willingly empathise – for example by synchronising your breathing, as described in the Introduction. It is very helpful if both bodies are synchronised because vital body massage is basically steered by the body's intelligence.

Seat yourself close to the person you are massaging, so that your writing hand is turned towards him or her. It is best if you sit back on your heels, parallel to the body of the person being treated, so that you can look in the direction of his or her head. You can stay upright in a relaxed position this way, and easily bend over forwards to carry out the massage. You will expend the least effort in this position, and remain internally collected. You can also always take a look at the face of the person concerned – direct feedback as regards the success of your massage.

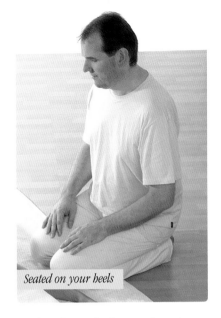

Seated on your heels

It is best if you take the crystal wand, crystal stylus or longish tumbled crystal (called the 'stylus' from now on) in your hand like a pencil, so that you hold it between thumb and middle finger and guide it with your index finger. The back of it will rest in the joint between thumb and index finger, if it is long enough (which would be ideal). You will need more power to hold and guide it if the stylus is shorter.

It is often easier to use the broader tip of the stylus initially, when making your first attempts with vital body massage. This end has – as already noted – a more relaxing and calming effect. Possible reactions to the massage are, therefore, more moderate. This is good at the beginning, because you still have to concentrate on the 'technique' of the massage and the various sequences. Go ahead and use the more pointed end once you feel more secure. The massage will be livelier then…!

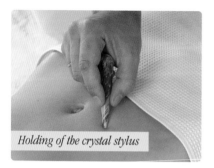
Holding of the crystal stylus

Now, to begin the vital body massage, place the crystal stylus on the skin very, very gently, and let it remain there for a moment. It is a minimal touch, with no pressure whatsoever; on the contrary: lean back a bit 'internally' just so you have the feeling you are pulling the stylus back, if you are in a leaning-forward position. Practise it on your own knee or thigh before the massage: sit upright, lean forward and place the stylus on your skin with a light pressure. Now move it gently in a circling motion a couple of times. And now lean back a few millimetres (more internally than externally), just as if you were laying a pen down at the end of writing a letter. The stylus stays in position, naturally, in this case, but you pull it back just enough so that you are barely touching the skin,

so that there is only a hint of a touch left. Can you feel the difference? Yes, exactly, that's it!

In vital body massage with healing crystals we 'hover' above the entire body, making small circles with the crystal stylus, just grazing the skin with a hint of a touch. More precisely: the 'circles' are actually small spiralling motions that, beginning at one point, get larger, and then return to this point in a spiralling motion. We wander over the whole body in a circling fashion, by relocating this central point. In doing so we keep changing the direction of motion – on impulse or whichever direction feels easiest!

It is possible to treat the vital body without any skin contact at all, but touching means that the attention of the person being massaged is directed to the relevant area, which improves the effect and keeps our counterpart spiritually present. The effect is more physical, meaning that it is more a stimulation of the reflex-zones, if contact with the stylus is harder. That feels good too, but it is a different massage form which needs a separate description (and may be included in a future book).

Motion of the crystal stylus

It is very important for massage of the vital body that contact with the stylus is really only minimal – very gentle, just a hint, even 'affectionate'! The gentler the better.

As long as you are in tune with your client, you can basically leave it up to your intuition to determine where to begin the vital body massage, and in which direction you would like to proceed. But do please remember to gradually massage the complete body. Even when focusing on some specific area, vital body massage is in principle a massage of the whole body, with the goal of harmonising the energy movements in the whole vital body. The beginning harmonisation might, in rare cases, become independent at a certain point and then cover the whole vital body, quite swiftly. This is experienced as a wave of wellbeing suddenly spreading throughout the person being massaged. The signs of this wellbeing are unmistakable: sudden relaxation, sparkling eyes or a blissful facial expression. Connoisseurs want to have more and more of this, of course. You still stop at this point – always leave when the party's at its height…

But we haven't come that far yet. You can either proceed intuitively or follow a certain sequence, at the beginning, as we have already said. The 'standard procedure' (which is rarely carried out) would begin with the client lying in the prone position; start at the crown of the head and then run down the neck, shoulders, back, buttocks and legs (one after the other) to the soles of the feet and the tips of the toes, using empathic/intuitive circling movements. Then, with the client supine, you change position and massage upwards starting at the tips of toes, then the feet, legs, pelvis abdomen and chest, along the arms to the fingertips and back (one arm after the other). The arms are stretched out to the side with palms upward as you massage from armpit to fingertips. The arms are then positioned loosely next to the body with palms down on as you massage back to the shoulders.

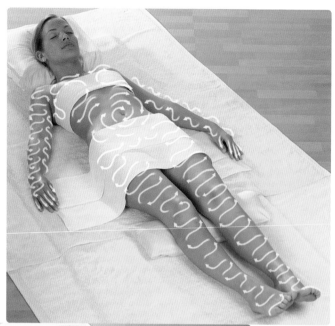

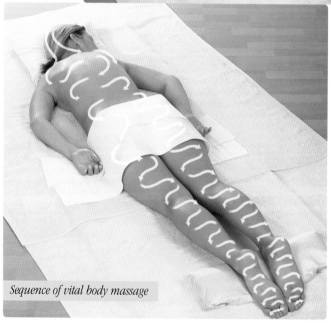

Sequence of vital body massage

Then change your position and sit above the head of the person you are massaging. You now proceed to massage from the shoulder along the neck and behind the ears up to the top of the skull (first one side, than the other) and from there over the forehead to the temples and ears, then from the base of the nose over the closed eyelids to the zygomatic bone and hinge of the jaw; and finally from the nose over the cheeks, around the mouth and over the chin. These 'paths' in the face are only clues, though! The procedure changes here intuitively all the time, according to what you are experiencing. At the end you can lay the crystal stylus on the 'third eye', the chakra point between the eyebrows, for about twenty to thirty seconds, and then end the vital body massage. Listen to your feelings here as you should do throughout the massage – a good conclusion brings grace to the whole process.

Sequence of vital body massage

Always allow yourself to be 'led' by the vital body when you apply the circling movements during a vital body massage. The best way to achieve this is through the attitude that it is not you 'making' the movement, but rather that you are just letting it happen.

If you have doubts, try switching hands, or changing to the other side, to see if it is easier to circle to the right or left for a moment. The easier movement is always the correct one. You will reach a free flow after a while and the movement will seem to take place by itself. Your hand simply circles clockwise one time, counter-clockwise the next, clockwise, counter-clockwise et cetera, while you are moving it over the body. You can basically just observe, and keep an eye on the whole process. Stay in contact, too, with the person you are massaging by simply watching him or her. Give emerging reactions their space as described in the Introduction. The vital body massage ends either after the completion of the massage of the whole body, or at a 'good point' (see above).

Vital body massage with stylus

It is best to stay present (spiritually and physically) initially, after the completion of the vital body massage. Just be quiet and be aware of how the person you treated is doing. As it is an ethereal massage it is very important that you 'trade back' energy that might have been exchanged, and that you free energy that might have got caught in the room, as we have discussed in the Introduction. This can be done mentally as long as you sit quietly waiting, next to the person whom you massaged. There is enough time afterwards for exchange, if desired, to cleanse the crystal stylus used, and to deliberately let go of your 'practitioner' role (see Introduction).

The vital body massage

1. Comfortable position for the person being treated; enough warmth
2. Have the crystal wands, stylus or other crystals and stones ready
3. Collection, protection and willing empathy
4. Upright posture, e. g. sitting on your heels, leaning forward slightly to treat
5. Hold the crystal stylus in your hand like a pencil
6. Lay the crystal on the skin very gently and circle delicately on impulse. Massage the entire body, alternating the circling directions
7. Let alternating spiralling movements happen – see which direction is easier, if necessary
8. Possible sequence of the massage: back of the head, back, buttocks, back of the legs, feet, front of the legs, pelvis, abdomen, chest, arms, head, face
9. Stay in contact, ask the treated person how he or she is doing as necessary
10. End the vital body massage at the completion of the massage of the whole body or at a 'good point'
11. Conclusion, stay present, observe and ask about needs
12. Trading back of taken-over energy and dissolving of energy still stuck in the room
13. Feedback and conversation if desired
14. Deliberate stepping out of the 'treating person' role
15. Cleansing of the crystal stylus, and clearing up of the room, if necessary.

What does vital body massage with healing crystals achieve?

Vital body massage with healing crystals increases the energy flow in the vital body, and thus improves communication within the organism as well as between the body, soul, intellect and spirit. In most cases, this is noticeable at first in an altered coenesthesia – an improved coenesthesia; but we might not notice this immediately. That is to say we become more clearly aware of the areas that are not all right once we become more aware of our whole body.

> Vital body massage doesn't make everything 'good' straight away. It does not work wonders, even though it feels wonderful. While it does tend to improve things for the better, it also shows the current status quo.

The improved communication between body, mind, intellect and spirit lets us suddenly understand more clearly what is good for us in different areas. That is why it is important to observe which needs and wishes arise in the period after a vital body massage – and to follow them! If we suddenly have an urgent wish to sleep, then we probably need it. So, off to bed! We sometimes do not even notice that our sleep disturbance has suddenly disappeared. It is worth following an urge, if we suddenly feel one: to do more sports, for a certain dish, certain hobbies, contact with certain people, the wish to talk things out or the urge to settle something. The things that suddenly show up after a vital body massage can suggest areas that lead to inhibition and blockages of the energy flow in our vital body in our daily routine – the appropriate impulses are often helpful for their solution.

The goal of this massage is the harmonising of the vital body. This is attained in the short term through the massage, but only stays stable if we shape our life harmoniously accordingly. The return to an inharmonious state shows us all those particular areas that are sources of disharmony; or maybe we have insights into what could prolong and stabilise this harmonious state. If we repeat vital body massages on a regular basis, they can contribute to a changing and reorganising of our life – as long as we follow through the respective impulses and implement them. The ability to implement them, too, is improved by vital body massage. The swirling and circling of the vital body indicates change, mutability and willingness to change. We strengthen our capacity to make changes in our life by supporting this turning and swirling. That is why vital body massages make you more flexible –

physically and spiritually. The massages make you more vital, because 'change is life', as Chinese medical science says (and life is change). You improve the energy flow and its balance, which, in turn, makes your life more balanced.

> A good image for the effect of vital body massage is water: it is versatile, mobile and can adapt to any form – and it still keeps its balance any time and anywhere effortlessly!

Physically, the improved vitality appears as more stable health. But not everything is 'good' here immediately: things that have to be changed show up here first, so that certain disorders appear, or become more readily discernible. A number of things can show up, layer by layer, until the blockages and disorders have dissolved. This process is made easier and simpler through vital body massage. The intensity of many disorders diminishes, and often all that is then needed is to keep watching as they dissolve.

We can now give the vitality a direction (on the physical, intellectual, mental and spiritual level) by adding certain healing crystals, such as wands, styluses or longish tumbled stones, to the vital body massage.

The results are predetermined by the nature and properties of the crystal, which can spread, establish and manifest its effects much better through this 'changing massage'. We should, therefore, think carefully about which crystal we choose. Always take the neutral rock crystal if there is any doubt, if you do not know, or are just unsure which crystal fits best. Rock crystal simply gives energy and creates clarity – and, as we have said, we can always benefit from that!

> Vital body massages with healing crystals have an effect that can be perceived immediately (sense of wellbeing, improved coenesthesia, spiritual freedom) and a medium- to long-term effect (flexibility, more stable health, 'new' ideas and impulses, new dynamics and order in life). The long-term aspects become stronger if we repeat the massage on a regular basis.

Which crystal stylus has which effects?

Specific experience exists for the following crystal types as wands, styluses or longish tumbled stones for vital body massage. This does not mean that these are the only healing crystals that can be used for this massage. This selection, though, is recommended especially for the introduction to vital body massage with healing crystals.

Agate is generally available as a crystal stylus, not as a wand. It is applied in vital body massage mainly for topics like protection, security, good sleep and a better 'connection to earth'. Vital body massages with agate impart inner security and stability. Physically, it assists digestion, excretion, connective tissue and skin.

Ametrine was available as a crystal wand in the past, but is harder to find today. Its qualities are similar to amethyst, but make you happier and more dynamic. Physically, vital body massage with ametrine is very good for the nerves.

Aquamarine is unknown as crystal wand or stylus and found very rarely as a longish tumbled stone. A lens-formed stone can be used here instead. Aquamarine gives lightness and serenity accompanied by discipline and endurance. That is why you have the feeling that things are accomplished 'in the blink of an eye'. Physically, aquamarine regulates growth and hormonal balance, and helps allergies, especially hay fever. Vital body massage with aquamarine also has a positive effect on the eyes, especially for crossed-eyes and short or long-sightedness.

Amethyst is mainly available as a crystal wand. **Banded Amethyst** (Chevron-Amethyst), which is also well suited for vital body massages is obtainable in stylus form and in the form of longish tumbled stones ('drops'). Amethyst gives inner peace and helps overcome mourning and grief. It relaxes, but makes you alert and aware at the same time. Physically, vital body massage with amethyst even eases strong tension and headaches.

Aventurine is available as crystal wand and stylus. Vital body massages with aventurine are excellent for problems with falling asleep. Aventurine helps to turn off the thoughts circling in your mind, as well as to diminish stress and nervousness. Physically, vital body massage with aventurine is very good for the influence of radiation, for example in sunstroke.

Calcite (orange) is available as a crystal wand and stylus. It imparts comforting warmth that strengthens confidence and trust in vital body massage. Physically, calcite is very good for growth and strengthens digestion, connective tissue, skin and bones.

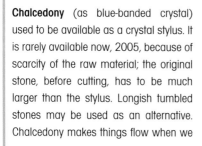

Chalcedony (as blue-banded crystal) used to be available as a crystal stylus. It is rarely available now, 2005, because of scarcity of the raw material; the original stone, before cutting, has to be much larger than the stylus. Longish tumbled stones may be used as an alternative. Chalcedony makes things flow when we feel inhibited and limited. It makes us open, communicative and alert. Physically, vital body massage with chalcedony boosts the flow of body liquids, especially lymph. The activity of the glands, kidneys and bladder is also often stimulated.

Fire Opal is not available as a crystal wand or stylus. There are, very rarely, longish tumbled stones of fire opal in bedrock that are ideally suited for vital body massage. Fire opal bestows wonderful erotic massages. It vitalises, makes one open-minded, cheerful and fond of life, and makes sexuality fun. Physically, it gives power and the capability to perform, boosts potency and fertility.

Fluorite (as multicoloured 'Rainbow Fluorite' from China) is a classic crystal wand and stylus. It is unfortunately very fragile, and therefore must be treated carefully. Fluorite gives (depending on the initial situation) structure and order to life or makes one more flexible, freer and more open. Vital body massage with fluorite also helps stress, learning and concentration disorders. Physically, it improves posture and mobility, and helps coughing, hoarseness and irritated or diseased mucous membranes.

Heliotrope is available as crystal wand. Vital body massage with heliotrope strengthens the ability to define oneself and to have a grip on life (or to get a grip on life). Physically it stimulates the immune system, which is the reason vital body massage with this crystal is very good for colds and the beginning of illnesses. It also has an easing effect in heart conditions.

Jasper (Red Jasper, Brecciated Jasper) can be found as crystal wands and styluses. Vital body massages with red jasper make one very active and dynamic. They give power and drive, but sometimes make agitated and impatient. Physically, they stimulate circulation and help constant weakness and fatigue.

Landscape Jasper is mainly available in the form of crystal styluses, rarely as wands. Yellow-brown landscape jasper gives quiet reliability and endurance (in contrast to red jasper). Physically, vital body massages with landscape jasper assist the digestion and excretion as well as the cleansing of connective tissue. They therefore ease allergies.

Magnesite is available as crystal wand and stylus. It has a relaxing effect and helps cramps and various pains. Vital body massages with magnesite make one patient and calms agitation and fearfulness. Physically, magnesite helps headaches, migraines, sore muscles, stomach disorders, nausea, backache and joint pains.

Obsidian (Snowflake Obsidian) is available as a crystal wand and stylus. It helps pain, mental and physical blockages as well as the consequences of accidents and injuries. The vital body massage stimulates circulation and gives internal warmth, if you have a tendency towards chilliness and cold feet and hands.

Onyx Marble has recently come onto the market as crystal wands and styluses. Onyx marble's effect is (internally) releasing in situations of constant challenge, and it is simultaneously calming and constructive in vital body massage. Physically it is very good for spinal problems, intervertebral discs, meniscus and joint conditions.

Rose Quartz is also one of the classic crystal wands and styluses. It makes one sensitive and empathic, encourages cheerfulness, helpfulness and empathy. Vital body massage with rose quartz helps many heart ailments (especially cardiac arrhythmia), sexual problems (caused by tension and pressure to perform) and boosts fertility.

Prase is sometimes available as a crystal stylus. It works very well for swelling, bruises and other pain, eases radiation effects, including sunburn and sunstroke, and helps heat sensitivity as well as the consequences of overheating.

Ruby-Kyanite-Fuchsite is a rarity as crystal stylus. This stone, composed of three minerals, eases tension due to stress and extreme pressure during vital body massage. It eases pain, encourages good sleep, gives serenity and the feeling of protection. Physically, it is very good for paralysis, rheumatism, infections, skin diseases, heart and back disorders.

Rock Crystal is the classic crystal wand and stylus. Longish tumbled stones are not rare either. It can be used practically universally as a neutral, clear quartz and can be unreservedly recommended for first experiments with vital body massage. Rock crystal simply gives the right amount of energy and stimulates clarity. Vital body massages with rock crystal are very liberating.

Rutilated Quartz is available as a crystal wand. Vital body massage with it loosens tightness, tension and anxiety and enhances the sense of a wide, free space. It also lightens moods, dissolves fears and gives a feeling of security and strength. Physically, rutilated quartz encourages cell regeneration and helps with many stubborn illnesses, especially bronchitis and illnesses of the respiratory tract.

Schorl (Black Tourmaline) is available as a crystal stylus and wand. Naturally-grown slim crystals are sometimes round-polished at the base for the latter. Schorl allows one to reduce internal tension and to become energetically more 'perm-eable'. Because of this it also helps to pro-tect against the influence of electro-smog and also against energetic and mental attacks. Massage with it balances ener-getic differences in the vital body, and strengthens it; giving a feeling of protec-tion. Schorl helps us be neutral in conflicts and makes us even-tempered. It eases pain and tension, in energetic terms unblocks scar tissue, and helps numb-ness.

Serpentine (often under the commercial name 'China-Jade') is available as a crys-tal wand and stylus. It helps with nervous-ness, restlessness, fluctuations of mood and the feeling of not being protected. Vital body massage with serpentine is very relaxing, and can therefore also help when it is difficult to reach orgasm as a result of tension. Physically, massage with this crystal helps cardiac arrhythmia, kidney, stomach and menstruation dis-orders.

Smoky Quartz is a classic crystal wand like the other crystal quartzes. It has been used as an anti-stress stone for a long time in vital body massage. Smoky Quartz quickly helps relieve tension caused by stress and pain, but at the same time also strengthens one's own ability to work under pressure so that one does not let oneself become stressed so easily. It also helps to compensate for radiation effects, and strengthens the nerves.

Sodalite is available as a crystal wand and stylus. Vital body massage with it is cooling, eases heat sensitivity, reduces fever and blood pressure and helps sore throats and hoarseness. Sodalite helps one attain the space and freedom to expe-rience what one would like to. It supports you in being true to yourself, to change behaviour patterns and to work consis-tently on your own development.

Tektite is available neither as a crystal wand nor a stylus. But as its natural form is a somewhat furrowed drop, it is also suitable, as such, for vital body massage. Tektite frees and helps to let go; massage with it also gives a strong feeling of freedom and detachment. Tektite can, therefore, be used particularly when we feel that we are ensnared by many things, and our life is too tight and suffocating because of this. Tektite also helps to compensate for the effects of electrosmog, and accelerates healing processes.

What else has to be taken into consideration for vital body massage?

What basically applies for all healing crystal massages applies here in particular: please do not give a vital body massage if you are not well yourself, or are not in a good mood! It is not only your hands which have an effect, especially in etheric massage, but also your moods and thoughts! A massage given when you are tired, reluctant or sick can weaken both of you – the person treating and the person being treated. Massage only if you are feeling well and if you feel like doing it. You can obtain wonderful results with vital body massage with healing crystals, as long as you observe the given rules. (These still leave you a great deal of freedom for your own intuition and creativity.) The 'path along the body' in particular is only a suggestion; it is not 'set in stone'. The speed and duration of the massage is also up to you. But one rule is unchanging:

> Never go against the natural direction of the flow of energy swirls in the vital body! Always follow the easier direction, or the direction in which it appears to flow on its own.

Bear in mind that, as we have already said, there is no 'good' or 'bad' regarding movements to the right or left. These are exactly as they are. And please follow them lightly and gently. You do not need to 'push'; in fact, move your crystal stylus like a blade of grass over water. Try doing this once, it only works if you do it lightly and gently.

The vital body massage will be a success if you follow these rules. You will need a little practice at first, but you will soon become confident in this relatively easy massage.

Not all stone types should be used during pregnancy. Experience shows that agate (pregnancy protection), amethyst (peace, relaxation), onyx marble (against back disorders), rock crystal (universal), calcite (bones, growth, development), chalcedony (for lymph congestion or oedema), heliotrope (differentiation, protection against infections), rose quartz (feeling for one another) and serpentine (relaxation) are all good stones to use. Please be careful in the last two months of pregnancy, though, if the pregnancy has not progressed smoothly. Vital body massages are recommended directly before birth, though, because they can facilitate birth. Magnesite or serpentine can help to relax the pelvic floor at this time, for example.

Prudence is also necessary if someone has been acutely or chronically ill. Vital body massages should only be administered by experienced doctors or complementary practitioners in this case. This applies, for instance, even to colds where there is a high fever. Some of the above-mentioned indications are therefore noted for such specialists. There are easier and safer methods for domestic purposes: for example, use a 'receiving' quartz crystal to bring down fever. More about this in the *Healing Crystals First Aid Manual* (Earthdancer Books @ Findhorn Press, autumn 2006).

If you would like to study vital body massage with healing crystals under expert guidance, contact Edition Cairn Elen (address in the appendix), for further information on where this massage is taught.

There is no reason not to apply a vital body massage if this type of massage appeals to you, you are in good health and mood, and the person you are treating is healthy to a large degree. Be happy about the exchange and the mutual touching as well as the possibility of doing good – and both of you enjoy the experience! Vital body massage is primarily a pleasurable treatment. Have fun!

Harmonising massage with amber

Hildegard Weiss

*Amber is unique.
As petrified resin, it has distinctly
different properties in comparison with crystals,
which are composed of minerals. That is why
massage with amber is a particular and
separate healing stone massage.*

Encounter with amber massage

Harmonising massage with amber came to my attention at a crystal healing symposium in Idar-Oberstein in 2002 when I visited a demonstration by Thorsten Vorbrodt. I was already familiar with healing crystal massages, and I had already got to know morphic field massage, among other things, in my training with Michael Gienger. I had also already tested crystals in massage with my clients for various ailments. The results had confirmed the effects of the crystals during the massage. So the suggestion of a special amber massage swiftly took root in fertile soil, given this background. And something new and complete evolved out of the sum of my previous experiences.

Harmonising massage

I always use a wide comfortable massage couch for treatments. My clients feel very good on it and my body retains the best possible relaxation while massaging in both sitting and standing positions. You can massage on the floor, of course, if you do not own such a bed. I always make sure that the temperature in the room is comfortable for the client, have a blanket handy and play quiet relaxing background music. I relax the client's knees with a knee-roll if desired, and place small amber pieces in both their hands for them to hold.

The massage itself begins at the feet, with the client lying on his or her back. I can massage seated in this position. The massage can be administered with or without massaging oil (jojoba, Saint John's wort, et cetera). With amber, the massage is often experienced as even more enjoyable with oil. I take both heels in my hands and become aware of the body rhythm through the breathing or through the pulse at the ankles. I attune myself to the rhythm, and relax the feet with various loosening-up exercises, if necessary (for example by rubbing the upper side towards the toes, circling the ankles with the fingertips, light pulling of the individual toes – both feet at a time, et cetera). The feet are subsequently placed back on the bed in as relaxed a state as possible, so that I can reach the bottom and inside of the foot comfortably. I massage the soles of the feet over the chakra zones with gently circling motions of the amber.

The 'easier' direction of rotation is always the 'right' direction – as we noted in vital body massage by Michael Gienger, above – with the circling motions of amber massage as well. Trust your instincts as you move the stones, to find the way in which it feels smoothest.

The chakra zones of the soles of the feet correspond approximately to the zones of reflexology massage. You can harmonise the individual organs with this massage.

Chakra zones of the soles of the feet

Crown chakra

Nose/forehead
Nose/forehead

Thymus *Neck/throat* *Neck/throat* *Thymus*

Heart *Heart*

Solar plexus
Solar plexus

Navel
Navel

Root
Root

Chakra zones of the soles of the feet

Possible abdominal noises confirm the relaxation of the individual organs. This is how you will know that contact with the client has been established, and the client will now relax visibly.

I massage both soles of the feet simultaneously, slowly and equally with the amber. Retain the massage direction as shown in the picture. The duration of the massage of the respective points is up to the individual. Trust your feeling, and observe your massage client's reactions.

You will follow with the massage of the back of the foot from the toes to the ankle; once again both feet simultaneously.

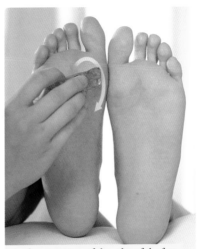

Amber massage of the soles of the feet

Pay special attention to the ankles – inside and out: they are gently encircled by amber.

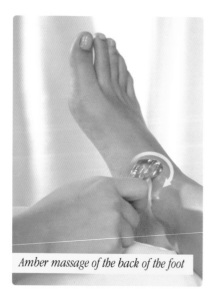

Amber massage of the back of the foot

Our attention to the knees activates circulation and dissolves possible waste products.

We now massage the thigh in the same way as we massaged the lower leg.

The amber pieces should be left resting in the middle of the thigh at the end of the massage. If they haven't been already, the legs should now be covered to hold the activated warmth.

Now the legs are massaged individually. The amber is left lying on the ankle of the resting leg; you might need to help it stay put with a towel. The other leg is now treated, from ankle to knee. I always try to stay in physical contact with my client with both hands. Before I start treating the second leg, I place the amber onto the knee of the leg I have just finished. It stays there until the second leg has been treated, with the amber that was on its ankle, as far as the knee. After that there is a piece of amber lying on this knee, too.

The knees will then be treated synchronously, once again with circling movements. Toxins that can sometimes lead to arthritis tend to particularly accumulate in the knee area.

Amber massage of the thigh

Subsequently, the hands and arms are now massaged with amber in the same fashion as the legs and feet: firstly, the palms of the hand from the carpus joint (wrist) to the tips of the fingers; secondly, the back of the hand to the carpus joint.

The amber rests on the carpus joint of one hand until the massage of the other hand is completed. Leave the amber on the wrist of the resting arm, and continue up the forearm of the other.

The next point of rest is at the elbow joint. We do not pay enough attention to the elbow joint. Just imagine if you had to work at the computer, or drive a car, without your elbow joints…

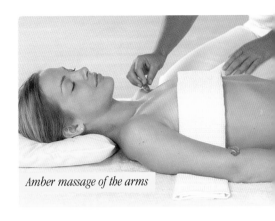

Amber massage of the arms

There are two advantages of setting a point of rest here:

1. We direct our attention to this important joint ('energy follows attention', in ancient shamanic wisdom)
2. We activate blood and oxygen distribution in this joint area with our light, circling, purposeful motions with amber.

Here we also leave a piece of amber on the first elbow joint while we massage the second one. Then a piece of amber rests on this elbow, and we continue on up the first arm in the same fashion to the shoulder.

The next point of rest is the shoulder joint and we leave a piece of amber here whilst we work on the second arm.

We pay particular attention to the shoulder joint with light, circling, purposeful motions with amber as well.

Our shoulder joints establish, among other things, the nerve connection between head/body and arms. The shoulder muscles also need our special attention. In writing, eating, turning our head, carrying something, sleeping, and so forth our shoulders are being used in each movement. It is not for nothing that we use the expression 'to shoulder something'!

So we have activated the energy in our limbs and guided it through our body up to the shoulders. We have also given the inner organs attention with the chakra massage of the soles of the feet.

We now turn to the easily-overlooked chest muscles and their ligaments with the next stage of the massage. We rub the area above the chest, to the shoulder joints, with amber in our hands.

Rubbing across the chest

Then follows the massaging of the neck muscles, on both sides of the neck, out to the shoulder joints. We do **not** massage the front of the neck because of the sensitivity of the larynx and thyroid gland.

I subsequently glide the flat of my hands under the supine upper part of the body of my client as far as I can. I then make fists and run them up to the shoulders along the spine. This action is very relaxing for a tense back. I repeat this a few times.

I now lay the amber onto the cheekbones and take my client's head into my hands very gently. It rests here for a while. Both my own and the client's attention is now directed to the head region. (The rest of the body can be covered if desired.) I then quietly and slowly take my hands away again and leave time for the client to notice the difference in the position of the

head. He or she can now enjoy the facial massage in a much more relaxed state.

Letting the head rest in the hands

I begin to rub the amber over the cheekbones towards the ears with small, circling motions.

Rubbing towards the ear with circling motions

I lay a stone on the chin after this. I massage from the tip of the nose to the hairline with another stone. The motion ends in the air! I prevent possible energy concentration in the head this way (the massage motions on the head are repeated several times, depending on the situation).

Then I proceed with both stones, beginning under the lips. I massage the lower jaw to the jaw joint, on both sides of the face, with gentle motions. I then begin on the upper jaw above the lips, and massage to the side towards the jaw joint.

The amber is then reapplied at the outer point of the eyebrows. I then massage around the eyes to the root of the nose, in small circles; from there along both sides of the nose downwards, over the corners of the mouth to the chin, and slowly back to the jawbone.

The next point of application is the root of the nose. I rub the forehead towards the hair line, synchronously.

Synchronous rubbing towards the hairline

I then lay the stones to one side and conclude the massage by gently pulling both earlobes at the same time.

Body contact is kept for a while by cupping my opened hands under the client's head at the neck. The client's deep inhaling and exhaling signals the point where the massage ends.

Now I let the client rest for at least eight minutes.

The sequence of a harmonising massage with amber

1. The chakra zones of the feet synchronously
2. Back of the feet and ankles synchronously
3. The right and left lower leg consecutively
4. Knee joints synchronously
5. The right and left thigh consecutively
6. The right and left hand, inside and outside, consecutively
7. Right and left forearm, including elbow, consecutively
8. The right and left upper arm, including shoulder joint, consecutively
9. Shoulders and chest area
10. The side and back of the neck
11. The facial zones
12. Let the client enjoy the sensation.

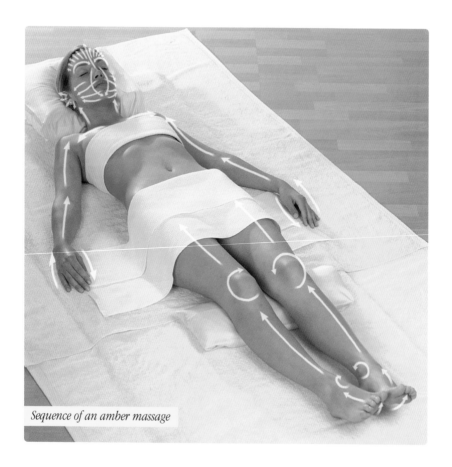

Sequence of an amber massage

This amber massage produces a feeling of circulating warmth in the body, with the result that 'too much' or 'too little' energy in the different body areas can be harmonised.

Amber is outstanding for this form of massage because of its special electromagnetic vibrations.

Amber loves a sunny place in twigs or tree cavities to 'refuel'. I also bathe it in a resonance bowl! Simply pour water into the bowl, put the amber into it and let the cleansing sounds resound.

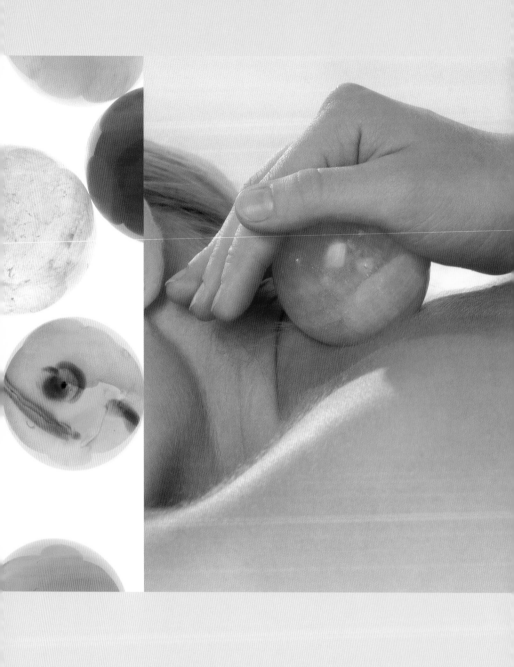

Massage with crystal spheres

Ursula Dombrowsky

*A massage with crystal spheres is
a body-oriented treatment with wide-ranging effects.
Massages with crystal spheres have an activating and relaxing effect at the same time, and encourage
a better body awareness (coenesthesia).*

Massage with crystal spheres

In this treatment our massage client is massaged by applying varied pressure in different directions with a crystal sphere. The massage is administered over the whole of the back, beginning in the hip area, adapting pressure as required. The whole body can be massaged in this manner, with a little practice. Muscles are relaxed and circulation is encouraged through massage with crystal spheres. Massages with crystal spheres have an activating and relaxing effect at the same time, and encourage a better body awareness (coenesthesia), and result in distinctly increased vitality. Physical blockages and their mental/spiritual origins can also be released in this fashion.

A physical blockage can have many causes. Sometimes it simply develops out of excessive demand on physical capabilities; often, though, emotional and spiritual issues are also part of the picture.

In the long run, it is not sufficient to treat the person only on one level. Good therapy will include the person in his or her entirety, and identifies and works with the flow of energy between spirit, soul, mind and body.

The emphasis is clearly on the body in massaging with crystal spheres, as blockages that have been compressed are found here. This has holistic effects, but is nonetheless a mainly physically-oriented treatment. If attention is directed to the body, its distinct language tells us what the human 'computer' has memorised.

Becoming aware of these things through the use of massage can give us an opportunity to adapt or change our life.

The body

The human body is an exquisitely complicated, living entity. Physique, movement and functions are interconnected, and dependent on each other.

Our body consists of a very complex system. It consists of billions of individual cells, and while we do not need to be concerned about, say, blood circulation, we are still able to be aware of what is going on even in our smallest toe. Our body functions in a fascinating manner, and yet most of the time without being appreciated to any great degree.

If you visualise a company with several employees and know how much communication is necessary to make things work and be harmonious, then you begin to realise how complex harmonious co-oper-ation is. You have to determine who is responsible for what, and meetings are necessary to ascertain the moment-by-moment status. Constant co-operation is necessary. If just one person does not co-operate, it has an effect on everyone, and the parent company too.

Our body is an enormously large organism with very many different areas. And it works very well, by and large. Do we value it enough, or do we take everything for granted?

It is generally only when our body doesn't work efficiently that we come under pressure to act, finally. Maybe we have not taken any notice of the subtle hints of small disorders, as we live our lives at such an active and hectic pace. There are so many ways to distract oneself...

We do not notice the hints of change early enough if we are not in our own centre any more.

Communication within the body

Communication of the cells with each other happens in various ways and at different speeds.

Blood circulation constitutes the slowest transportation. The entire hormonal system's messages, the white and red blood cells, the haemorrhaging factors as well as the nutrients are brought to the different areas of the body through the circulation of the blood. The oxygen that is transported

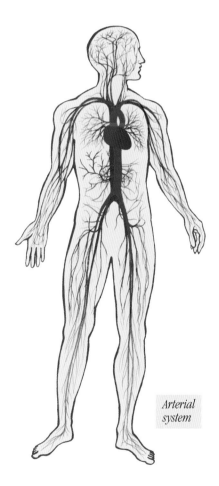

Arterial system

in the blood is needed by every cell to be able to fulfil its function. It is jointly responsible for the burning of nutrients and for metabolic processes. Waste and carbon dioxide are also removed in the blood.

Secondly, the nervous system also transmits information. These electrical impulses are transmitted to the individual cells extremely swiftly. We can perceive their speed when we have burnt our finger, for example. There are three types of nerve tissue:

◎ The vegetative nerves cause physical activity such as, for example, gland or organ activity, at an unconscious level
◎ The motor nerves communicate motor impulses
◎ The sensory nerves communicate sensation (sense of touch, temperature, pain et cetera).

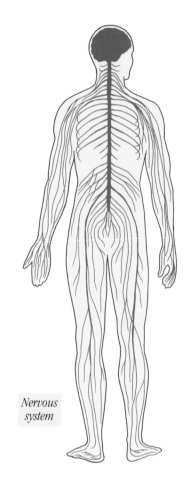

Nervous system

The nerve fibres pervade our whole body in a similar way to the branches of a tree. They originate in the brain and run to the outer layers of our skin through the spinal cord.

The exit point of the fascicles (bundles of nerve fibres) is located between the respective vertebral bodies. An accumulation of ganglia is located next to the spine, from this the nerves then lead to the rest of the body and the extremities.

Particular fascicles supply specific areas of the body. Each is responsible for an area of skin, a muscle area and an organ system. If a blockage occurs in any one of those areas it will show up in the other areas too, in due course, because an altered nerve impulse now streams through the other supply area.

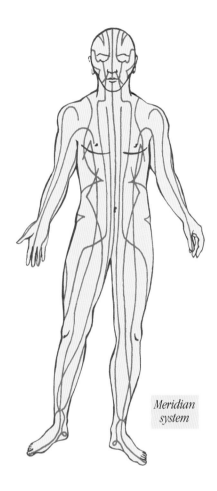

Meridian system

Scars and energetic blockages can disturb the energy flow here.

Lastly, the body also communicates through the biophotones (light impulses), direct cellular communication.

These complex communications systems overlap each other in manifold ways and are deeply connected, clearly demonstrating that no influence in the body remains 'only' at a local level; it always spreads out through the whole body, and finally reaches our soul, mind and spirit.

The third information flow takes place in the meridian system. These energy channels have been known, and been used to heal, in the Far East from time immemorial. The meridians are connected to certain organs, but also pervade certain regions of the body. Information is always transmitted in both directions in the meridians.

The musculoskeletal system

Humans would be totally incapable of moving without the musculoskeletal system: that is without bones, joints and muscles.

An adult human has approximately two hundred bones, and movement is possible due to the two hundred and seventy-seven twin and three single skeletal muscles.

The arbitrary skeletal muscles, the muscles that submit to our will, often show our disposition. Our muscle tone has a tendency to be too high if we are 'tense' in general. Our muscles will probably be tense somewhere if we approach something tensely. It usually shows in the top part of

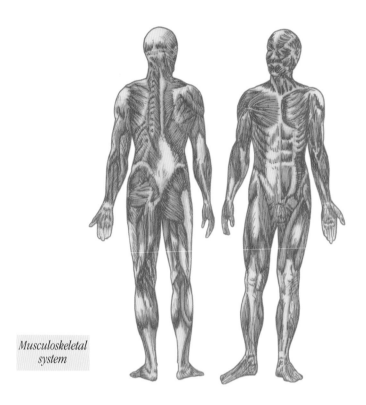

Musculoskeletal system

our back (almost as if we have been carrying a heavy backpack the whole time) if we have taken on a burden that's too heavy, or if we cannot let go of our daily affairs.

Physically, a certain hard-headedness shows as a hard neck. This often does not pertain to our transient and changing body of thought, but rather to our fundamental inner attitude. The muscles have lost their suppleness if pain and tension are now present. This means that the energy supply of the individual cells may decrease. Metabolic waste will then be left in the cell, the

cells ability to exchange is reduced, and so on. The result is that supplying the cell is made even more difficult. This is where the massage is applied.

Blood circulation can be improved and and muscles made more supple through purposeful massage.

Spine and Pelvis

The spine is our axis of life. We walk upright and move thanks to its flexibility. It constitutes the middle point between the left and right sides of our body.

> Our pelvis is our foundation, our horizontal centre. An imbalance here has consequences for our advancing (or legs), as well as for our climbing or growing (or spine).
>
> This is why the pelvis and the spine play such an important role in massage with crystal spheres.

Body rhythm

It is not just our inner attitudes that show up at the body level. Effects also result from our environment and our activities. *We do not, most of us, have the time any more to live with a certain consistency or in a more or less constant rhythm.* Our sleeping behaviour, for example, has been changed in a very distinct way by the influence of the media and artificial light.

Often our body is unable to regenerate enough at night. We, generally, have a sleep rhythm that is too short; we also have not done enough spiritual preparatory work, because we have not taken time for reflection during the day. It is very good and helpful for sleep and therefore the body if we find a way to review the day in the evening without distraction, closing the things that have happened, and becoming aware of what is still open. Then we do not have to take care of these reflections in our dreams, and the body receives more energy to regenerate it because we are able to sleep better.

This is the reason that sleep before midnight is known as 'beauty sleep': it has to do with the detoxification and regeneration of the body during the night.

> If the body cannot detoxify and regenerate optimally at night, it can result in residues and possible accumulation of toxic burdens.

Myogelosis (areas of hardening) can develop, for example, in the muscles. These can be loosened effectively with massages and by drinking enough pure water – and, of course, with enough sleep.

> Crystal massages are of great benefit, and can improve many different states of the body and mind. The effects can only be permanent, however, if they are incorporated into a healthy way of living, a gentle rhythm of life, a balanced diet, good sleep, the capability to change inner attitudes, and, last but not least, the pursuit of meaning and fulfilment in one's life. Massage with spheres, especially, can help things that need to be changed to flow again, and open up new perspectives hand-in-hand with conscious changes to one's life.

Be careful: massages with spheres continue to have an effect after the massage is over!

What are the origins of massage with crystal spheres?

I work with various body-oriented massages in my practice. These include, among others, classical massages, spinal mobilisation, meridian therapy and energetic work. Crystal healing became an additional part of my therapies a few years ago when I was looking for a connection between these various disciplines. Crystal spheres came to my attention, and this massage developed out of my explorations with them. I received very good responses after just a few initial treatments. I found I could disperse tension very easily, and the body awareness (coenesthesia) of my clients improved noticeably. Many clients became aware of amazing connections with which they could change their life habits, both during and after the massage. A reduction of their previous tension was the consequence.

I worked with three different crystal spheres in the beginning (additional explanations of the various crystals will follow later). Since then I have used fifty different types of crystal. This makes the massage more personal.

The sequence of movements with crystal spheres

The most important motion when massaging using a crystal sphere is the horizontal figure-of-eight. The figure-of-eight is the symbol of infinity. It also has a harmonising effect on both halves of our brain – the figure-of-eight is used to assist the balancing of the left and right hemispheres of the brain in kinesiology. It consists of two complete circles that touch each other, each circle depicting a whole.

Building up a feeling for massage with crystal spheres

Take a sphere between your hands and rotate it to get a good feel for massaging with crystal spheres. Notice how the sphere moves in your cupped hands.

Try out for yourself how massage with a crystal sphere feels by, for example, massaging your thigh. Vary the pressure and be aware of how this feels and also what level of pressure you enjoy.

We work with 'adjusted' pressure in physical massage. This means that we go up to the bearable threshold of pain. More pressure is usually possible than one can imagine in the beginning.

How is the massage administered?

A warm and quiet room that smells good is best for a massage. You can give the massage on the floor or on a couch. The person being massaged should only be wearing underpants. Lay enough blankets on the floor and cover the person being massaged, so that they can be comfortable. Having the room warm enough means the person can relax more easily.

The motto is: the more comfortable the position, the more enjoyable the massage.

The person lies on his front to have his back massaged. It sometimes feels more comfortable if a pillow is placed under the stomach. This results in relaxation of the lumbar region and the small of the back. This position is important if a heavy lordosis (curvature of the spine to the front) exists. A rolled-up towel or a blanket can be placed under the ankles, if necessary.

Any crystal that is available as a sphere is suitable to use when massaging. A sphere with a diameter of between three and five centimetres is adequate. The smaller the sphere the smaller the area being massaged and the less pressure needed. When using a larger sphere the skin area and the receptors under it are touched more superficially. If you would like to try this out on yourself, then press down on your skin with the tip of your finger, and then, in comparison, with the entire surface of your thumb. Do you feel the difference?

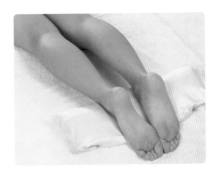

Massage with spheres is performed directly on the skin. Massage oil is not needed, because the massage is more effective without oil.

The inner attitude

The best help you can give the person you are treating is that you are 'present' for him or her, and that you act only as a catalyst for their improving health. There is no sense in taking over the blockages or problems of another person. Everybody is responsible for his or her life, and also for making changes within him- or herself. The body can often regulate a physical disorder itself after an external impulse has set events in motion. That is why it is good if you remain aware of yourself and your boundaries, and aim simply to be quietly present.

In addition there are various ways in which you can protect yourself:

◎ Through words, by saying a prayer or a protective phrase

◎ By visualising yourself wrapped in light

◎ By using aromatic or Aurasoma oils, for example – putting them on your hands and then moving your hands over and around your body without actually touching it in order to create a protective shield

◎ By tapping your hands before the massage and becoming more aware of your own body in this way

Having done your own personal preparation and protection you can then tune into the person lying in front of you.

Remember that the massage you are about to give is to make the person you are treating feel better and more relaxed.

It is important for this treatment that you focus your full attention on the person you are massaging. Work with an appropriate degree of pressure in the introductory part of the massage. It is sometimes necessary to apply pressure up to the pain threshold when freeing blockages, but never over it. A steady increase in pressure is more enjoyable than starting off the massage with heavy pressure; remember to always apply a suitable amount of pressure during this stage of the crystal massage.

Selecting a
crystal sphere

There are various ways of selecting the appropriate crystal sphere. You can approach it in a playful manner if you have more than one to choose from. (If you only have one sphere just simply use this one.)

◎ It might be even better if the person you are massaging selects his or her own sphere, because it is their body that is going to be treated. The person can feel which crystal is 'right' by holding their hand over the spheres with their eyes closed. This feeling might show up in the form of a tickling sensation, a feeling of warmth, of coolness, or simply by the person touching the right

crystal. The desire to select a certain sphere will simply be there.

◎ You can also count your spheres and ask the person to be treated to give you a number, then you simply take the corresponding sphere.

◎ Another possibility is that the person selects the sphere that appeals to him or her most at that moment – or the one that appeals to him or her least at that moment. Either crystal could turn out to be very appropriate.

◎ You could also offer to choose the sphere for the person you are going to massage yourself. To do this you can refer to the crystal information that follows.

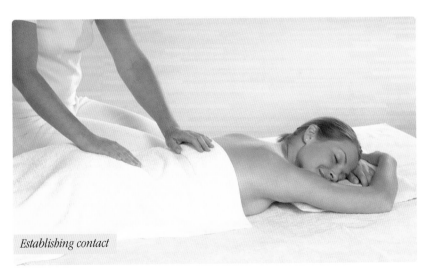

Establishing contact

Beginning the crystal sphere massage

Start by standing or sitting next to the left hand side of the person to be treated and establish contact.

Introduction at the pelvic area

A massage with crystal spheres begins in the pelvic area. You experiment with pressure levels here; be sure to give enough time and attention to this area. The more you can bring balance to this area the easier it will be to continue and develop the massage.

The sphere is guided with the right hand. Place the sphere carefully onto the sacrum. The hip and dorsal area is massaged using

the motion of a horizontal figure-of-eight. The centre or the crossing point of the eight is always located in the spinal area, between the individual vertebrae.

The buttock muscles are then massaged firmly, between five and seven times. The sphere can also be guided in circles in this area. A good level of pressure is appropriate here because the buttock muscles usually contain a lot of tension build-up.

Then return to the bottom of the back and massage in figure-of-eight movements again. Work up the entire spine in figures-of-eight, making sure that the loops of the eight always cross at the individual vertebrae. It is important to adapt the pressure here so that it feels good to the person being massaged.

Spine/figure-of-eight motion

The entire spine is worked over in the direction of the cervical vertebrae this way. The goal is to balance the right and left sides of the body.

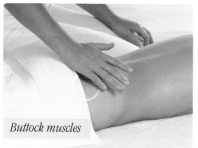

Buttock muscles

A little trick that can help if someone turns out to be ticklish is to take his or her hand and place it on their back. The person then feels as if the treatment is being carried out by his or her own hand. And tickling yourself just doesn't work!

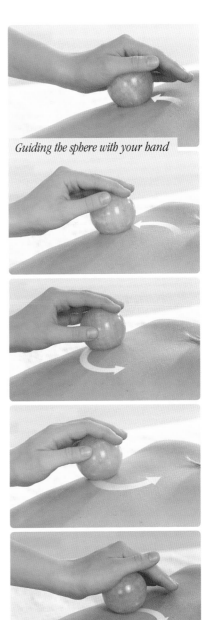

Guiding the sphere with your hand

Tickle stop

It is important to adapt the pressure of the massage so that no additional tension is caused because the person being treated will stiffen up if unnecessary pain is felt. This should clearly be avoided!

There is a so-called healthy pain, though, that whilst it hurts you also helps your body to relax.

> The whole hand guides the sphere, with palm and fingers used in tandem.

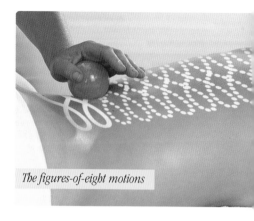

The figures-of-eight motions

Continuation of the massage with crystal spheres

Massage next to the spinal column and over the back muscles on the left side, starting from the neck area. Use a circling motion that leads downwards in the direction of the hip area. The circles are not large, only 3 to 5 centimetres in diameter.

Once you have done this massage the muscles on the right side of the back using the same circular motions you used on the left side of the body.

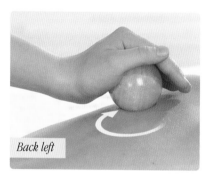

Back left

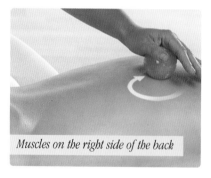

Muscles on the right side of the back

Once you have arrived at the hip, massage up the spinal column again in figures-of-eight.

Now massage the side muscles. You can apply firm pressure near the shoulder blades, but lighter touch is required between the ribs.

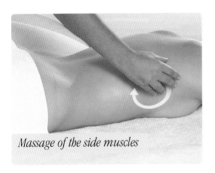

Massage of the side muscles

It is easier to massage the shoulder area if you change your position. Stand or sit at the top of the body; this enables you to work on this area systematically. Take your time here and massage the entire shoulder area, using small circles. Adapt the pressure here as well, so that it is perceived as having a loosening effect.

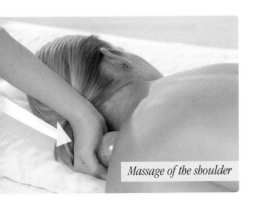

Massage of the shoulder

Choose a posture for yourself that means you do not have to massage with your arm at an angle. The pressure is then applied more directly and can be administered better.

We continue from the shoulder to the muscles at the nape of the neck, which are also massaged at length, to loosen what can be strong tension in this area little by little.

Nape of the neck

Up until now the spheres have been guided in your cupped hand. There is a different grip for the next, more energetic, part of the massage. The sphere is now placed on the spinal column and is held between the thumb and index finger, using the bent middle finger to guide it.

Position yourself on the right side of your client.

Starting at the nape of the neck the middle finger now pushes the sphere down the back slowly and lightly. When you reach the hip level lift the sphere and replace at the nap of the neck next to the spine and roll it down to the hip once again parallel to the first roll. The sphere is rolled in this way, length by length, until the entire width of the back has been treated.

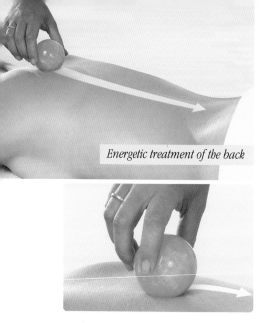

Energetic treatment of the back

The sphere helps to activate energy flow in the direction it is moved in, and you will be able to see where energy is still blocked. The movement of the rolling sphere can change strongly here: it can move lightly and freely, become inhibited and slow down, or even appear to stop. Experiencing these sensations requires a certain amount of practice, but they can be very exact indicators of where energy is blocked.

This energetic work is always carried out in the direction of the meridians, in the direction of the legs whilst working on the back.

It is good to repeat the massage of blocked areas or areas where the energy is not flowing freely, several times. The energetic rolling from the neck in the direction of the buttocks should be repeated and the results monitored. You can end the treatment as soon as the sphere rolls smoothly at the point where it was 'sticking'; or you can continue with the massage of the whole body. A creative game develops between sphere and user— for the wellbeing of the person being treated!

You might feel thirsty after giving a massage. It is good to drink a glass of water or two after giving a treatment.

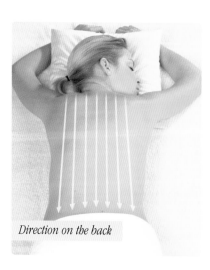

Direction on the back

What does the crystal sphere massage achieve?

Massage with crystal spheres is very good for relaxing muscles and to encourage blood circulation in the tissues. This can appear as a feeling of warmth, a tingling, or even a feeling of lightness. A pleasant feeling of heaviness can also develop – you get a of sense the body and what it needs. Rotating the sphere allows you to massage with stronger pressure, so that deeper muscle layers can also enjoy the massage. Therefore massage with crystal spheres is both liberating and loosening.

Massaging with spheres encourages the balancing of the left and right hand sides of the body.

Different aspects are attributed to these two sides. The right side stands for the masculine principle: intellectual, active, future-oriented. It also suggests authoritativeness, assertiveness and goal-orientation.

The left side stands for the feminine nurturing nature: intuition, the past, patience and an ability to relate to people and situations.

We can work with both our intuition and our intellect if the right and left side of the body are in harmony. A blockage can also build up just on one side of the body, either the emotional or the intellectual side, depending on our inner attitude. We always treat both sides of the body when giving a crystal massage!

The primary purpose of a massage with spheres is to strengthen energy flow so that blockages can be released. An awareness of your own inner body attitude can also result from a massage. Generally an enhancement of body awareness (coenesthesia) can be observed.

Indications and Contraindications

Massage with crystal spheres can be applied for: tension (of an acute or chronic nature), inner feelings of stress, fatigue, muscle cramps, backaches, balance, after a hectic day, as something good to do for a partner, as a health precaution and for many similar reasons or conditions.

You should abstain from a massage with spheres if strong acute pain exists, if strong pain develops suddenly, after a jerky movement, if transmission or perception disorders exist in the extremities, in the case of open wounds, or immediately after an operation.

If you are not sure whether it is appropriate to give a massage, consult your client's doctor or complementary practitioner.

Which crystal should you use for a massage?

A distinct connection between the type and locality of the existing tension and other phenomena and an intuitively chosen crystal has long been established. You can basically use any crystal that is available as a sphere. People always find the stone suitable for them.

Therefore, I've included only a small selection of the crystal spheres most commonly used in my massages up to now, including any effects and reactions I have observed. This is definitely not a comprehensive list, but should help to differentiate the focal point of the spheres.

Agate imparts the wonderful awareness of one's skin being a protective covering. It is soft and comforting. Agate assists in building up protection and helps you to help yourself. It brings a feeling of security, allowing you to let go. Agate fortifies, strengthens and helps you work better under pressure.

Amethyst is very effective against tension. It loosens cramped muscles, and can also be used to treat headaches. It has a relaxing and rather cooling effect, which is why it can be very helpful after over-exertion.

Amazonite is very helpful if you have too many burdens resulting in tension and pain. It helps the body find peace. It has a relaxing and pain-relieving effect.

Ametrine imparts a beautiful sense of harmony to the body. It calms nerves and brings inner peace, whilst simultaneously making you feel awake and lively. It brings exactly the right balance between tension and relaxation. Ametrine has a strongly uplifting effect, and can therefore be useful at times of unhappiness, tension or discontentment.

Apatite can be very usefully for physical exhaustion. It has a strengthening and constructive effect. Apatite can be helpful for posture disorders, and is good for bones and joints.

Aventurine is good if the skin is sensitive or irritated. It can also help mentally if you are irritated, nervous, anxious and tormented by constantly circling thoughts. It can also be used when lack of rest from stress has resulted in blockages in the body.

Calcite (orange) is a sunny, strengthening crystal that gives very good coenesthesia

and strengthens one's acceptance of oneself. It tightens tissue, mobilises muscles and strengthens bones. Calcite is also good for massaging children who have growing pains.

Chalcedony as a blue-banded crystal offers assistance to the body in getting everything flowing again. It is also appropriate for tightness of the skin. It lightens the spirits and stimulates conversation.

Chrysocolla has a balancing effect, and is harmonising for all areas of the body. It brings intellect and intuition into harmony, balances mood fluctuation, and smoothes muscles, tissues and skin. It is also very good for the healing of scar tissue. Chrysocolla can also be stimulating for the digestive system if the hip and buttock areas are massaged well.

Epidote is a very good crystal for fatigue, especially fatigue cause by long illness or mental strain. Therefore a very good constructive and strengthening massage can be given with Epidote.

Fluorite makes you physically and mentally agile: it loosens energetic blockages, clears the head and is good for joints, bones, cartilage, tissue and skin. This is why fluorite can support you if you are trying to change your posture.

Jasper, especially in its red crystal form, has an inspiring, strengthening and vitalising effect. It helps to support and strengthen you if you are going through a difficult time. Jasper stimulates blood circulation and warms you if you have a tendency to feel cold. A massage with this crystal is activating, so it is better not to use it for a massage too late in the evening.

Labradorite has a cooling effect if you are hot-tempered and a warming effect if you are too cool. It frees the tissues of waste and sediment and therefore also helps rheumatic pain. Labradorite helps you to become aware of the origins of any physical disorders.

Lapis Lazuli makes you open, self-assured and self-confident. It gives you a sense of space if you feel constricted allowing the body to be calm but responsive. Lapis Lazuli can stimulate you to hold inspiring conversations after the massage.

Magnesite relaxes, calms and eases cramps. It is good for the muscles and connective tissue in a crystal sphere massage. Magnesite helps you to let go and eases headaches. It can also be used as part of a detoxification regime.

Obsidian is very good for pain; it also helps after trauma or an operation either to heal after surgery, or after consultation with a doctor! Massage with Obsidian loosens energetic blockages.

Malachite is particularly good for women, as it relieves cramps and works on menstrual problems. It makes sense to massage intensively with this sphere in the lumbar and sacral bone area for these problems. Malachite brings back memories and therefore helps one realise the cause of existing blockages.

Ocean Agate (Ocean Jasper) is very good for a constructive massage. It has an uplifting and motivating effect and is very good for engendering strength and peace in hectic times, or after an illness.

Nephrite is a good crystal to strengthen the kidneys; this will show up in a better flow of energy. It helps the body to thoroughly detoxify.

Onyx Marble (Aragonite) is very good for strain, and makes one loose-limbed and aware of one's body. Onyx Marble helps in disorders of the back, spine and vertebrae. It is important to position the patient correctly when massaging with Onyx Marble (put a pillow under the stomach!).

Pressure has to be applied very carefully in the spinal area.

Rock Crystal can be used very effectively in any situation. Rock crystal has a vitalising and harmonising effect on both the left and right halves of the body. Because of its strengthening effect it can help you become more conscious of your body.

Petrified Wood helps you to feel a general sense of wellbeing, both within your body and in the external world. Petrified Wood improves your relationship with your body, it can sometimes help if someone is overweight and at times when you do not like yourself. It has a warming effect, and is therefore good for cold limbs.

Rose Quartz is a good crystal for harmonious and affectionate treatments. It allows the body to be calm and relaxed and encourages one's awareness.

Rhodonite is a very good crystal with which to massage scar tissue. It can help the tissue become smoother again. It also helps one be more motivated and active.

Rutilated Quartz has a liberating and vitalising effect, especially for the chest and heart area if you massage the upper back intensively. It can, therefore, be used when one feels constricted. Rutilated

Quartz stimulates the regeneration of tissues and therefore helps in chronic health conditions.

Smoky Quartz is a good aid if there is tension in the back area that needs to be dispersed. It is very effective as an anti-stress crystal.

Tiger Iron gives vitality and energy for life. It encourages blood circulation and haematopoiesis, and helps with extreme fatigue. Tiger Iron lets you feel vigorous and strong again. It is better not to massage with Tiger Iron too late in the evening – its effect is so stimulating that you might not be able to sleep.

Stromatolite has a very good effect on the digestion. Massage the bottom part of the back intensively to help the digestion in this way; as it helps one to 'let go' it has a detoxifying effect.

Tourmalin as black **Schorl** is very good for the energy flow through the nerves. That is why it can be used to improve body sensations. It can also be used to treat scar tissue; however, it can take a lot of time to treat this.

What else has to be taken into account for crystal sphere massages?

The massage should be administered in a quiet constant rhythm. The person being massaged can become very anxious and nervous if the treatment is carried out too quickly or frenetically.

To ensure this, choose a gentle rhythm and speed, one that enables your client to relax, on the one hand, and will stimulate circulation on the other.

It is possible to massage the whole body, but be very careful in the abdominal area. It is important that you take into account the position of the colon, which begins in the lower right abdomen, then ascends on the right and runs across to the left side of the abdomen between the navel and the solar plexus. It descends down the left hand side of the body.

This is the reason we always massage in a clockwise direction when we work on the abdomen: this assists the flow of movement through the intestines.

The abdominal area is the area where deep feelings are situated; this means that a lot of feelings can arise when we massage the abdomen. This is why I recommend that when massaging the abdominal area only a very light pressure is used and you will need to have a great deal of trust in each other.

Another possibility is that the patient massages their own abdomen.

However, just as with all other forms of massage you will only learn by doing!

So just take heart and try out the massages – or take advantage of some of the training courses and possibilities in which you can learn to massage under the instruction of experts. (More about this in the appendix.)

The authors

Michael Gienger

Michael Gienger worked as a shiatsu masseur before he became involved in crystal healing at the end of the eighties. Massaging with crystals has been part of his life for twenty years and he has shared his experience and knowledge through seminars and training courses for ten years. This work is now being continued by his colleagues in the Cairn Elen Life Schools. Today, Michael Gienger primarily works as an author, editor and publisher. The emphasis here is on natural studies, philosophy and healing, especially crystal healing.

Michael Gienger is joint founder of the Stuttgart Crystal Healing Research Group (1988), Steinheilkunde e.V. (1995), as well as the Cairn Elen Life Schools (1997) and the Cairn Elen Crystal Healing Network (1998). He was also involved with the project 'Minerals in Medical Science', which brought together science and the healing experience, from 1997 to 2002. Michael

Gienger is also known for four books he has published in English: *Crystal Power Crystal Healing* (Cassell Illustrated, 1998), *Healing Crystals* (Earthdancer @ Findhorn Press 2005), *Crystal Massage for Health and Healing* and *The Healing Crystals First Aid Manual* (both Earthdancer @ Findhorn Press 2006).

You can learn more about Michael Gienger and his projects from:
www.crystalhealing.de
www.michael-gienger.de
www.edelstein-massagen.de
www.cairn-elen.de

Hildegard Weiss

Hildegard Weiss lives and works in the

Crystal Healing Centre in Grünebach, on the border of Siegerland and Westerwald. She enjoys encouraging people to live in accordance with nature. She offers lectures, workshops and courses, as well as health counselling with Bach flowers or astrology. Relaxing massages that further awareness of our body and its needs and that are attuned to the individual client are standard parts of her repertoire.

Her knowledge comes from many years of study with Michael Gienger (crystal healing), Dr. Wighart Strehlow (the teachings of Hildegard von Bingen), and Daniel Agustoni (craniosacral therapy), amongst many different teachers of crystal healing and massage techniques, in addition to her studies at the school for alternative healing. Her desire is to show people that a mindful interaction with their body, mind and spirit results in more *joie de vivre* and bliss.

Hildegard Weiss is always being instructed and supported on her path of practice by her Buddhist *sangha* in Hohenau (Bavaria), who live by the guidelines of the Zen master Thich Nhat Hanh. Training in this practice is also offered at her centre.

More information and programmes of seminars and lectures can be obtained at PRISMA, Hildegard Weiss, Hauptstrasse 7, 57520 Grünebach, Germany
phone: +49 2741 22218
fax: +49 2741 932 9485
prismaww@hot-mail.com
homepage: www.prismaww.de

Ursula Dombrowsky

Ursula Dombrowsky has a diploma in medical massage and reflexology. She has been fascinated by crystals since childhood.

She has immersed herself in this field since her first crystal healing seminar in 1998. Today she combines crystal healing with manual and energetic physical and speech therapy in her practice.

Ursula Dombrowsky started crystal healing courses for children during her three years of study at the Cairn Elen Life School. Her first book *Wenn Steine erzählen [When Crystals Tell Stories]* (Neue Erde Verlag 2003) grew out of this, along with her experience with her crystal-enthusiast daughters.

Apart from her work as masseuse and therapist in her own practice, Ursula Dombrowsky also offers crystal healing seminars and training, in which she teaches massage with crystal spheres, morphic field massage and other crystal healing topics. Her crystal healing elementary and main trainings conform to the guidelines of Michael Gienger and the Cairn Elen Life Schools.

Contact:
Ursula Dombrowsky, Büelgass 26,
8625 Gossau, Switzerland
phone and fax: +41 1936 2114
ursula@dombrowsky.ch
homepage: www.dombrowsky.ch

Information on crystal healing

Research, information and customer services

Steinheilkunde e.V.
Crystal Healing Research Project
Unterer Kirchberg 23/1
88273 Fronreute, Germany
Tel: +49 7505 956451
Fax: +49 7505 956452
info@steinheilkunde-ev.de
www.steinheilkunde-ev.de

Internet information
www.crystalhealing.de

Seminars and training

Crystal healing and crystal massage
Crystal counselling, seminars, elementary and main courses in crystal healing, crystal massage and related fields.

Cairn Elen Life School, Tübingen
Annette Jakobi, Mozartstrasse 9
72127 Kusterdingen, Germany
Tel: +49 7071 538266
Fax: +49 7071 38868
annette@edelstein-massagen.de
www.edelstein-massagen.de

Cairn Elen Life School, Swabian Alps
Dagmar Fleck
Rossgumpenstrasse 10
72336 Balingen-Zillhausen
Germany
Tel: 49 7435 919932
Fax: 49 7435 919931
info@cairn-elen.de
www.cairn-elen.de

Cairn Elen Life School, Odenwald
Franca Bauer, Berlinerstrasse 1a
64711 Erbach, Germany
Tel: 49 6062 919762
Fax: 49 6062 919763
franca@cairn-elen.de
www.cairn-elen.de

Crystal massage, crystal therapy, individual therapy
Wide range of training courses in various crystal massages, crystal therapies and natural healing methods. Will also be a training centre for individual therapy, tutored by Rainer Strebel.

Akademie Lapis Vitalis, Im Osterholz 1
71636 Ludwigsburg, Germany
Tel: 49 7141 441260
Fax: 49 7141 441266
info@lapisvitalis.de
www.lapisvitalis.de

Reflex zone massage with healing crystals
Institute, practice, lectures, seminars and training in reflex zone therapy. Also with crystal stylus.

Ewald Kliegel & Thomas Gutsche GbR
Rotenbergstrasse 152, 70190 Stuttgart
Germany
Tel: +49 711 264780, Fax: +49 711 2629578
info@reflex-zonen.de
www.reflex-zonen.de

More on crystal healing, further publications, events, seminars and training under
www.crystalhealing.de

More on crystal massage under
www.edelstein-massagen.de

Crystals as a natural experience

Exhibitions of our Earth's Treasures
The 'Steinzeiten' ('Stone Times') exhibition will give you a unique insight into the world of crystals. Here, the emphasis is on experiencing the power of crystals, rather than on the classification and display aspects characteristic of museums. Usually it's only miners who have

the privilege of seeing druses (crystal crusts lining caves, and so on); here you too can experience this; or you can journey into the past through gigantic fossil beds; or witness for yourself the power of crystals in meditation rooms. This exhibition will ensure you are touched by your fascinating encounter with crystals.

Steinzeiten, Rödingsmarkt 19
20459 Hamburg, Germany
Tel: +49 40 36900318, Fax: +49 40 36900310
info@steinzeiten.net
www.steinzeiten.net

Crystal examination and identification
Mineralogical/gemmological examinations
Authenticity examinations of minerals, crystals and rocks. Acquisition of gemmological tools and identification aids.

Institut für Edelstein Prüfung (EPI)
Bernhard Bruder, Riesenwaldstrasse 6
77797 Ohlsbach, Germany
Tel: 49 7803 600808, Fax: 49 7803 600809
lab@epigem.de
www.epigem.de

Edition Cairn Elen

"After Elen had accomplished her wandering through the world, she placed a Cairn at the end of the Sarn Elen. Her path then led her back to the land between evening and morning. From this Cairn originated all stones that direct the way at crossroads up until today."*

(From a Celtic myth)

'Cairn Elen'* is the term used in Gaelic-speaking areas to refer to the ancient slab stones on track ways. They mark the spiritual paths, both the paths of the earth and that of knowledge.

These paths are increasingly falling into oblivion. Just as the old paths of the earth disappear under the modern asphalt streets, so also does certain ancient wisdom disappear under the data flood of modern information. For this reason, the desire and aim of the Edition Cairn Elen is to preserve ancient wisdom and link it with modern knowledge – for a flourishing future!

The Edition Cairn Elen in Neue Erde Verlag is published by Michael Gienger. The objective of the Edition is to present knowledge from research and tradition that has remained unpublished up until now. Areas of focus are nature, naturopathy and health, as well as consciousness and spiritual freedom.

Apart from current specialised literature, stories, fairytales, novels, lyric and artistic publications will also be published within the scope of Edition Cairn Elen. The knowledge thus transmitted reaches out not only to the intellect but also to the heart.

Contact
Edition Cairn Elen, Michael Gienger, Stäudach 58/1, D-72074 Tübingen
Tel: +49 (0)7071 - 364719, Fax: +49 (0)7071 - 388 68,
eMail: buecher@michael-gienger.de, Website: www.michael-gienger.de

[1] Celtic 'cairn' [pronounced: carn] = 'Stone' (usually placed as an intentional shaped heap of stones), 'sarn' = 'Path', 'Elen, Helen' = 'Goddess of the Roads'

* Cairn Elen: in British ancient and contemporary Celtic culture, cairns are generally intentionally heaped piles of stones, rather than an individual stone such as a boulder or standing stone.

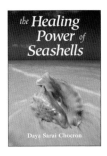

A quick guide to Seashells and their healing powers for everyone. This ancient Hawaiian wisdom is simple to understand and easy to put into practice. Included for your easy reference are photographs of Seashells and relevant descriptions to help you identify them. Most of the Seashells featured can be found on shores all over the world, and many are available for sale. This colourful book will immediately transport you to the beach!

Daya Sarai Chocron
The Healing Power of Seashells
Paperback, 96 pages, ISBN 1-84409-068-X

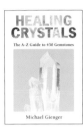

All the important information about 430 healing gemstones in a neat pocket-book! Michael Gienger, known for his popular introductory work 'Crystal Power, Crystal Healing', here presents a comprehensive directory of all the gemstones currently in use. In a clear, concise and precise style, with pictures accompanying the text, the author describes the characteristics and healing functions of each crystal.

Michael Gienger
Healing Crystals
The A - Z Guide to 430 Gemstones
Paperback, 96 pages, ISBN 1-84409-067-1

There are two types of angels: those with wings, and those with leaves. For thousands of years, those seeking advice or wanting to give thanks to Mother Nature have walked the ancient paths into the sacred grove. Because today sacred groves have become scarcer, and venerable old trees in tranquil spots are hard to find when we need them, Earthdancer is pleased to present this tree oracle to bring the tree angels closer to us all once more.

Fred Hageneder, Anne Heng
The Tree Angel Oracle
36 colour cards (95 x 133 mm) plus book, 112 pages
ISBN 1-84409-078-7

Other publications by Earthdancer

1   2   3   4   5   6   7   8   9   10   11   12   13   12   11   10   09   08   07   06

Crystal Massage for health and healing
Michael Gienger

This English edition © 2006 Earthdancer Books
English translation © 2006 Tom Blair
Editing of the translated text by Roselle Angwin,
   Carol Shaw

Originally published in German as *Edelstein-Massagen*

All rights reserved. No part of this book may be reprinted or reproduced or utilised in any form or by any electronic, mechanical, or other means, now known or hereafter invented, including photocopying and recording, or in any information storage or retrieval system, without permission in writing from the publisher.

World copyright © 2004 Neue Erde GmbH,
   Saarbruecken, Germany
Original German text © 2004 Michael Gienger

Cover photography: Amber Massage
Photo and concept: Ines Blersch
Cover design: Dragon Design UK
Photo and concept by Ines Blersch, www.InesBlersch.de
Photo models: Michaela Wersebe, Steven Kieltsch
Casting: fischercasting.de Stuttgart

Photos, concept and picture editing by Ines Blersch
Book design and graphical photo editing:
   Dragon Design UK
Typeset in ITC Garamond Condensed

Printed and bound in China

ISBN 1-84409-077-9

Published by Earthdancer Books, an Imprint of :
Findhorn Press, 305a The Park, Forres IV36 3TE,
Scottland.
www.earthdancer.co.uk . www.findhornpress.com

For further information and book catalogue contact:
Findhorn Press, 305a The Park, Forres IV36 3TE, Scottland.
Earthdancer Books is an Imprint of Findhorn Press.

tel +44 (0)1309-690582 fax +44 (0)1309-690036
info@findhornpress.com www.earthdancer.co.uk www.findhornpress.com

EARTHDANCER

A FINDHORN PRESS IMPRINT